IN SEARCH OF
THE OBVIOUS

IN SEARCH OF THE OBVIOUS

The Antidote for Today's Marketing Mess

—————

JACK TROUT

WILEY

JOHN WILEY & SONS, INC.

Published by John Wiley & Sons, Inc., Hoboken, New Jersey
Published simultaneously in Canada.

For general information on our other products and services or for technical support, please
contact our Customer Care Department within the United States at (800) 762-2974, outside
the United States at (317) 572-3993 or fax (317) 572-4002.

Wiley also publishes its books in a variety of electronic formats. Some content that appears in
print may not be available in electronic books. For more information about Wiley products,
visit our web site at www.wiley.com.

Library of Congress Cataloging-in-Publication Data:

Trout, Jack.
   In search of the obvious : the antidote for today's marketing mess / Jack Trout.
      p. cm.
   ISBN 978-0-470-28859-7 (cloth)
   1. Marketing.   2. Advertising—Brand name products.
   I. Title.

   HF5415.T729 2008
   658.8—dc22

                                                                            2008016815

Printed in the United States of America

10 9 8 7 6 5 4 3 2 1

To Richard Maggiore
The man who introduced me to Obvious Adams

CONTENTS

Preface   xiii

CHAPTER 1.   In Search of the Obvious   1
              This is the most important chapter in the book.
              It is simple, profound, and contains a secret that
              few know of . . . and someone else wrote most of it.

CHAPTER 2.   What Gets in the Way of the Obvious   11
              There are forces at play that don't make the search
              easy or sometimes even possible. They tend to
              obstruct clear thinking. Some forces are external.
              Some are internal. They all are things of which you
              must be aware. Forewarned is forearmed.

CHAPTER 3.   The Internet Can Be an Obvious Problem   25
              Nothing in the marketing and business world has
              received so much hype. But be careful, it is not the
              ultimate solution. It's about new ways to reach people
              with your obvious idea. It's just another tool but it can
              confuse things.

CHAPTER 4.   Advertising People Can Be an Obvious
              Problem   39
              Unfortunately, most advertising people look for the
              creative, not the obvious. For them, the obvious is

too simple and not clever enough. The old guard—Leo
Burnett, David Ogilvy, and Bill Bernbach—understood
this. The new guard, whomever they are, don't.

CHAPTER 5.   Marketing People Can Be an Obvious
              Problem   57
              Marketing people often don't appreciate what
              they should be focusing on. Most get hopelessly
              entangled in corporate egos and complicated
              projects. It's no wonder that the job tenure of
              a chief marketing officer is less than two years.

CHAPTER 6.   An Obvious Look at the Marketing Process   67
              If marketing people are to do a better job, they have
              to have a clear understanding of the marketing
              process—what's important and how to evaluate
              and operate the functions in which they are in
              charge.

CHAPTER 7.   Some Help in That Search for the Obvious   93
              The search should generally start with the
              competition. It's not what you want to do. It's
              what your competition will let you do. Also, you
              have to avoid making the kinds of mistakes often
              made. I'll also share two of my favorite
              obvious strategies.

CHAPTER 8.   You Must Be Aware of Some Obvious
              Ground Rules   129
              In another book, I wrote about the laws of
              marketing. A number of these are very important
              in the search for the obvious. Ignore them at
              your own risk.

CHAPTER 9.   Some Observations about Obvious
              Marketing Problems   151
              This chapter outlines the obvious ideas that
              could be used to solve some highly publicized
              marketing problems. Some are observations.
              Several were searches for the obvious that
              I conducted.

CHAPTER 10.   The Future Is Never Obvious   187
              A search for the obvious is about today, not
              tomorrow. You cannot predict the future and you
              should never try. Today is today. Tomorrow is
              tomorrow.

Epilogue   191

Bibliography   195

Index   199

*"Those who cannot remember the past
are condemned to repeat it."*

George Santayana
(1863–1952)

There's a lot of history in this book and people always ask me why I bring up old case histories to teach a lesson.

My response is that Mr. Santayana's advice is of great importance, as the past tells you what to do today. (Vietnam pretty much told us what would happen in Iraq.)

So it is in marketing. I tell young marketing people to study the past and to avoid thinking that the world is different. It isn't—because the human condition is the same.

In addition, this study has to focus on the long view as history unfolds slowly.

Why? Well it takes awhile to discover the truth. You have to carefully keep track of the results. There's a lot of ego in most business decisions so the truth is often hidden and few want to admit a mistake. As Mark Twain so artfully wrote, "You can't get the truth out of people until they are dead and dead a long time."

Jack Trout

PREFACE

Business is in an era of killer competition. And at a time when the function of marketing is of critical importance, marketing is in a mess.

I didn't appreciate how bad things had become until I came across some research as I was updating my book *Differentiate or Die*. (It became Chapter 2.)

In great detail, this study illustrated that while categories are expanding thanks to the Immutable Law of Division, something sinister is happening. Despite all the attention paid to branding these days, more and more of these categories are sliding into commoditization. In other words, fewer and fewer of the brands in these categories are well differentiated. In people's minds, they are there but that's about all. You could call them placeholders. They are sort of like squatters. They live there but don't own a meaningful idea that makes them unique.

Differentiation, of course, exists, and does so on the basis of a product or service actually owning values—real or perceived, rational or emotional—and occupying a real place in the consumers' minds—beyond the consumer just being aware of them. And the degree to which they possess these values and have meaning in the consumers' lives determines whether they have differentiated themselves. But fewer and fewer products and services are able to demonstrate any degree of actual differentiation.

To prove this, BrandKeys, Inc., a New York based loyalty and engagement research consultancy, conducted an analysis of 1,847 products and services in 75 categories via their Customer Loyalty Engagement Index.® Using a combination of psychological inquiry and factor regression, and causal path analyses, they were able to predict how positively or negatively consumers will act toward the products depending on their degree of differentiation.

On average, the study found that only 21 percent of all the products and services examined had any points of differentiation that were meaningful to the consumers. This is nearly 10 percent less than a benchmark study that was conducted in 2003. (There's more on this in Chapter 3.)

What this means is that more and more products are being sold on price—not benefits—which is not a happy place to be.

It's no wonder that chief marketing officers (CMOs) have a shorter job tenure than NFL coaches. The latest reports have them barely getting beyond two years before they are gone. As *BusinessWeek* commented in an article on the subject, "The job is radioactive."

Now here's the irony: While CMOs are being fired and U.S. brands are descending into chaos, confusion, and commoditization, U.S. consultants are producing book after book about what should be done about the mess. Seth Godin, a popular guru, calls for the need to be "remarkable," which sounds like being different. But "Purple Cows," which he espouses, are hard to breed in most corporations. W. Chan Kim and Renee Mauborgue talk about avoiding head-to-head competition by sailing out into a "Blue Ocean Strategy." (That sounds a lot like what I wrote years ago, that is, it's better to be first than to be better.) But "Blue Oceans" are hard to find these days. And what do I do in a sea of competitors?

Some concepts come and go very quickly. Nobody talks much anymore about excellence or Six Sigma or long tail or game theory. Some ideas, such as "Green Marketing" become instant fads thanks in large part to Al Gore.

Book after book sets out to get the authors out on the speaking circuit with concepts like "Lovemarks," or "Brandscendence," "Emotional Branding," "Buzz," or "BrandJam." Endless articles are written about the new generation of consumers who have "new mindsets" or "cravings." This leads to advice about "modes of entertainment" or "making loose connections" or "going inward" or "giving back." It all sounds like we're turning marketing into a new form of religion.

Finally, on top of all that, you have all the computer and Internet-generated research that makes things not clearer but more complicated. You can easily sum it all up by observing that marketing is increasingly becoming a complex science of data mining, number slicing, niche segmenting, and on and on. As I said, marketing is a mess.

This book is an effort to clear up all this confusion—to get back to what you should be looking for in solving any marketing problem. And it comes with no jargon, no numbers, no complexity. Many of my observations come from a bimonthly column I write for Forbes.com. Others come from my many years of writing on this subject. Some are new ideas. A search for the obvious has always been at the heart of my work. Why repeat myself? When people get it, I'll stop.

You'll notice that a few marketers such as Coca-Cola and General Motors and Volkswagen come in for some rough treatment. I'm not trying to be mean but, because of their visibility and history, they present wonderful lessons learned the hard way. Lessons you don't want to repeat.

Interested? Read on and learn from the ride.

CHAPTER 1

In Search of the Obvious

This is the most important chapter in the book. It is simple, profound, and contains a secret that few know of . . . and someone else wrote most of it.

Whenever I travel around the world, I'm often asked the same question: "What are your favorite books?"

Well, I'm going to let you in on a secret. The best book that I have ever read on marketing is one that was written over 90 years ago in 1916. And here's the good news. It is only 40 pages long, it contains no jargon or graphs or complex research. In fact, it's more like a pamphlet. Now the bad news. It's not easy to find and could be called a collector's item.

The book is titled: *Obvious Adams. The Story of a Successful Businessman* and it's written by Robert R. Updegraff. The book was an instant hit and a reviewer wrote in the *New York Times*, "The young man who is going to seek his fortune in the advertising business should have *Obvious Adams* for a handbook. Indeed, any young man who is going to seek his fortune in anything might be aided by the common sense and business acumen displayed in this little volume."

Why do I like this book so much? Because the search for any marketing strategy is the search for the obvious. Consider the dictionary definition of the word *obvious*: Easy to see or understand; plain; evident. With that definition, you begin to see why an obvious strategy is so powerful. It's simple, easy to understand, and evident. That's why it works so well.

Interestingly, when presented with a simple, obvious strategy, many clients are not impressed. They are often looking for some clever, not-so-obvious idea. What I often hear is something like, "That's something we already know. Is the solution that simple?" I then have to go into my "evident speech" which goes like this: "You're right, it is evident. But if it's evident to you, it will also be evident to your customers, which is why it will work."

Updegraff warned of this reaction when he wrote, "The trouble is, the obvious is apt to be so simple and commonplace that it has no appeal to the imagination. We all like clever ideas and ingenious plans that make good lunch-table talk at the club. There is something about the obvious that is—well, so very obvious!"

To give you a taste of Updegraff's wisdom, here are his guidelines in that search for the obvious.

Five Tests of Obviousness

THE FIRST TEST OF OBVIOUSNESS I borrowed from Kettering of General Motors, who had it placed on the wall of the General Motors Research Building in Dayton:

This problem when solved will be simple.

The obvious is nearly always simple—so simple that sometimes a whole generation of men and women have looked at it without even seeing it. Whereas if an idea is clever, ingenious, or complicated, we should suspect it. It probably is not obvious.

The history of science, the arts and the great developments in the world of business, is a history of men stumbling upon simple solutions to complex problems. Mr. Kettering's wise proverb might be paraphrased: "The solution when found will be obvious."

THE SECOND TEST OF OBVIOUSNESS is a question:

Does it check with human nature?

If you do not feel pretty certain that your idea or plan will be understood—and accepted—by your mother, wife, brothers, sisters, cousins, your next-door neighbor, the man who works at the next desk or machine, the mechanic who services your automobile, your minister, your barber, the manager of the grocery store where your wife shops, the person who shines your shoes, your Aunt Mary, your secretary, your seat-mate on the 5:29 suburban train, your most outspoken friends—if you don't feel comfortable about explaining your "obvious" idea to these people—it probably is not obvious.

These people will see it in its simple reality, uncomplicated by professional or technical knowledge, and free of the inhibitions that grow out of experience.

Collectively, they are a cross-section of human nature, and human nature makes or breaks any plan or nullifies the solution to any problem. It is the controlling factor in life and business, in science and the arts.

Whether it involves selling things to people, enlisting their support, getting them to follow a particular course of action, or inducing them to change a long-time habit, if your way of doing it does not conform to human nature, you will waste your time, money and energy to try to accomplish your purpose.

The public is curiously obvious in its reactions—because the public's mind is simple, direct and unsophisticated.

THE THIRD TEST OF OBVIOUSNESS is:

Put it on paper.

Write out your idea, plan, or project in words of one or two syllables, as though you were explaining it to a child.

Can you do this in two or three short paragraphs, so that it makes sense? If not, if the explanation becomes long, involved, ingenious—then very likely it is not the obvious. For, to repeat, "When you find the answer it will be simple."

No idea or plan, no program or project is obvious unless it can be understood and worked by people of average intelligence.

Often the attempt to express an idea or outline a plan on paper will automatically show up its weakness or complexities. Sometimes doing this will show you what is wrong with your thinking, and lead you to a simple and obvious solution. Certainly, putting it on paper is a quick way of showing you what you have—or haven't.

THE FOURTH TEST OF OBVIOUSNESS is:

Does it EXPLODE in people's minds?

If, when you have presented your idea, outlined your solution to a problem, or explained your plan, project, or program, people say, "Now why didn't we think of that before?" you can feel encouraged. For obvious ideas are very apt to produce this "explosive" mental reaction.

In many instances, from that moment on the whole matter appears to be settled, without further explanation or argument. It is just too obvious to need prolonged consideration. Even with such a reaction, however, it is usually wise to reserve [your] decision for a day or so. For sometimes there are hidden flaws which only show up after a night's sleep.

If an idea or proposal does not "explode," if it requires lengthy explanation, and involves hours of argument, either it is not obvious, or you have not thought it through yourself and reduced it to obvious simplicity.

Mental "explosions" are revealed in what people say, in the light that spreads over their faces, in the acceptance that comes into their eyes, when they grasp an obvious idea. It is one of the infallible tests of obviousness.

THE FIFTH TEST OF OBVIOUSNESS is:

Is the time ripe?

Many ideas and plans are obvious in themselves, but just as obviously "out of time." Checking the timeliness is often just as important as checking the idea or plan itself.

Sometimes the time may have passed, definitely and irrevocably; in which case the obvious thing to do is forget your idea. In other instances its timeliness may be ahead, which calls for patience, plus alertness.

The president of one of the big rubber companies once showed me his "Cupboard of the Future" where were stored many unusual articles made wholly or partially of rubber which were ahead of their time. These articles had been developed in the company's research laboratories, but as of then were too costly to compete with the same articles made with other materials. So they were being kept "on the shelf" until the price was competitive, either through the development of cheaper production methods, or through the rising costs of competing articles. (Some of the products in this cupboard have since been marketed successfully and are today quite commonplace.)

Next to the first test—the simplicity requirement—the timeliness test is perhaps the most important check on the obviousness of a plan or program.

"One of the cardinal virtues," wrote Emerson in his Journal, "is timeliness. My neighbor, the carriage maker, all summer is making sleighs, and all winter is making light, gay gigs and chariots for June and August; and so, on the first days of the new season, is ready . . ."

To be ready is to be timely; and to be timely is an obvious requirement.

After having read all that common sense, you might be thinking that it is indeed all too simple for today's times.

Well, the rest of this book will take you for a trip through the current business world to show you that what Robert Updegraff wrote in 1916 is still very meaningful today. In fact, when you consider marketing's mess, it's even more meaningful. But, before that, let's pause and talk about common sense and how it will help you in your search.

Common Sense Is Your Guide

Abraham Lincoln offered some brilliant advice on figuring out what to do: "You must draw on language, logic, and simple common sense to determine essential issues and establish a concrete course of action." Unfortunately, business executives often leave their common sense out in the parking lot when they come to work.

Common sense is wisdom that is shared by all. It's something that registers as an obvious truth to a community.

Simple ideas tend to be obvious ideas because they have a ring of truth about them. But people distrust their instincts. They feel there must be a hidden, more complex answer. Wrong. What's obvious to you is obvious to many. That's why an obvious answer usually works so well in the marketplace.

One of the secrets of the buzzword gurus is to start with a simple, obvious idea and make it complex. A *Time* magazine commentary on a Stephen Covey book captured this phenomenon:

> His genius is for complicating the obvious, and as a result his books are graphically chaotic. Charts and diagrams bulge from the page. Sidebars and boxes chop the chapters into bite-size morsels. The prose buzzes with the cant phrases—empower, modeling, bonding, and agent of change—without which his books would deflate like a blown tire. He uses more exclamation points than Gidget.

The dictionary definition of *common sense* is "native good judgment that is free from emotional bias or intellectual subtlety." It's also not dependent on special technical knowledge.

In other words, you are seeing things as they really are. You are following the dictates of cold logic, eliminating both sentiment and self-interest from your decision. Nothing could be simpler.

Consider this scenario. If you were to ask 10 people at random how well a Cadillac would sell if it looked like a Chevrolet, just about all of them would say, "Not very well."

These people are using nothing but common sense in their judgment. They have no data or research to support their conclusion. They also have no technical knowledge or intellectual subtlety. To them a Cadillac is a big expensive car while a Chevrolet is a smaller, less expensive car. They are seeing things as they really are.

But at General Motors (GM), those in charge would rather see the world as they want it to be rather than as it is. Common sense was ignored and the Cimarron was born. Not surprisingly, it didn't sell very well. (And we're being kind.)

Was this a lesson learned? It does not appear to be so. GM came back with the Catera, another Cadillac that looks like a Chevrolet. Like its predecessor, it didn't sell very well because it made no sense. You know it and I know it. GM didn't want to know it.

As Henry Mintzberg, professor of management at McGill University, said, "Management is a curious phenomenon. It is generously paid, enormously influential and significantly devoid of common sense."

Leonardo da Vinci saw the human mind as a laboratory for gathering material from the eyes, ears, and other organs of perception—material that was then channeled through the organ of common sense. In other words, common sense is a sort of super sense that rides herd over our other senses. It's a super sense that many in business refuse to trust.

Maybe we should correct that. You don't have to just be in business to ignore simple common sense. Consider the complex world of economists, a group that works hard at outwitting simple common sense.

There is nothing economists enjoy more than telling the uninitiated that plain evidence of the senses is wrong. They tend to ignore the human condition and declare that people are "maximizers of utility." In econo-talk, we become "calculators of self-interest." To economists, if we all have enough information we will make rational decisions.

Anyone who's hung around the marketing world for a while realizes that people are quite irrational at times. Right now, we're overrun by four-wheel-drive vehicles designed to travel off the road. Does anybody ever leave the road? Less than 10 percent. Do people need these vehicles? Not really. Why did they buy them? Because everyone else was buying them. How's that for "rational"?

The world cannot be put into mathematical formulas. It's too irrational. It's the way it is.

Now some words about intellectual subtlety.

A company often goes wrong when it is conned with subtle research and arguments about where the world is headed. (Nobody really knows, but many make believe they know.) These views are carefully crafted and usually mixed in with some false assumptions disguised as facts.

For example, many years ago, Xerox was led to believe that in the office of the future everything—phones, computers, and copiers—would be an integrated system. (Bad prediction.) To play in this world, you needed to offer everything. Thus, Xerox needed to buy or build computers and other noncopier equipment to participate in this on-rushing automated world.

Xerox was told it could do this because people saw the company as a skilled, high technology company. (This was a false assumption.) People saw it as a copier company.

Twenty-five years and several billion dollars later, Xerox realized that the office of the future is still out in the future. And any Xerox machine that can't make a copy is in trouble. It was a painful lesson in technical knowledge and intellectual subtlety overwhelming good judgment.

Finally, some thoughts about a business school education, which seems to submerge common sense.

By the time students finish their first year, they already have an excellent command of the words and phrases that identify them as MBA wanna-bes. They have become comfortable with jargon like "risk/reward ratio," "discounted cash flow," "expected value," and so forth.

After a while, all this uncommon language overwhelms critical thought and common sense. You get the appearance of deliberation where none may exist.

Ross Perot, in a visit to the Harvard Business School, observed, "The trouble with you people is that what you call environmental scanning, I call looking out the window."

To think in simple, commonsense and obvious terms, you must begin to follow these four guidelines:

1. *Get your ego out of the situation.* Good judgment is based on reality. The more you screen things though your ego, the farther you get from reality.

2. *Avoid wishful thinking.* We all want things to go a certain way. But how things go is often out of our control. Good common sense tends to be in tune with the way things are going.

3. *Be better at listening.* Common sense by definition is based on what others think. It's thinking that is common to many. People who don't have their ears to the ground lose access to important common sense.

4. *Be a little cynical.* Things are sometimes the opposite of the way they really are. That's often the case because someone is pursuing his or her own agenda. Good common sense is based on the experiences of many, not the wishful thinking of some.

Executives should trust their common sense. It will lead them to the obvious.

CHAPTER 2

What Gets in the Way of the Obvious

There are forces at play that don't make the search easy or sometimes even possible. They tend to obstruct clear thinking. Some forces are external. Some are internal. They all are things of which you must be aware. Forewarned is forearmed.

The Search Begins and Ends with the Chief Executive Officer

If top management isn't involved, chances are you won't get anywhere in your search for the obvious. In the old days, your big company chief executive officer (CEO) was far behind the firing line. When things went bad, there were people to be blamed and asked to leave. But today, it's a different story. The buck stops at the office of the CEO.

And it's not an easy job, which is why so many CEOs have unwillingly left their jobs in recent years. The truth is many

11

big company CEOs are barely in control of their company's fate, much less their own. There is a growing legion of competitors coming at you from every corner of the globe. Technologies are constantly changing, threatening your core business, and forcing you to transform. The pace of change is faster than ever before. George Fisher at Kodak tried to adapt but it doesn't appear that Kodak will find much happiness in the digital age.

It is increasingly difficult for CEOs to digest the flood of information out there and make the right choices.

But it can be done.

The trick to surviving is knowing *where* you are going. That's because no one can follow you (the board, your managers, your employees) if you don't know where you're headed.

Many years ago in a book called *The Peter Principle*, authors Lawrence Peter and Raymond Hull made this observation:

> Most hierarchies are nowadays so cumbered with rules and traditions, and so bound by public laws, that even high employees do not have to lead anyone anywhere, in the sense of pointing out the direction and setting the pace. They simply follow precedents, obey regulations, and move at the head of the crowd. Such employees lead only in the sense that the carved wooden figurehead leads the ship. (p. 68)

If there's one lesson about the search for the obvious that real leaders need to understand, here it is:

Success or failure is all about perceptual problems and opportunities in the marketplace. And it's all about understanding that the perceptions in the mind of the customer are where you win and lose.

Remember, the obvious idea must explode in the mind.

You cannot be swayed by those wonderful presentations by your executives on how your company can make a better product or leverage your distribution better or create a better way to get your salesforce into the marketplace. You have to stay focused on adapting to the mind of the prospect, not trying to change it. Minds are difficult if not impossible to change. And if your executives say it can be done, don't believe them. The more you understand the minds of your customers or prospects, the less likely you will get into trouble.

I once asked an ex-CEO of General Motors if he ever questioned the proliferation of models that eventually destroyed the meaning of the company's brands. (He was a financial man with little background in marketing.)

That question caused him to stop and ponder for a few seconds. His response: "No, but I do recall thinking that it was getting a little confusing." His concern was absolutely correct but he failed to act on his instincts. His assumption was that his executives knew what they were doing. This turned out to be a false assumption. But it took a number of years for this mistake to be felt at General Motors. Today, thanks to intense competition, mistakes are felt in a matter of months, not years. That's why marketing is too important to be turned over to an underling. To survive, a CEO has to assume the final responsibility of what gets taken to the marketplace. After all, his job is on the line.

Let's say you've focused on your competitors and figured out their strengths and weaknesses in the mind of the target audience. You have searched out that one attribute or obvious differentiating idea that will work in the mental battleground.

Then you have focused all your efforts to develop a coherent strategy to exploit that idea. And you have been willing to make the changes inside the organization to exploit the opportunities on the outside.

You must be willing to take the time to let that strategy develop. Marketing moves take time to develop so you must, even in the face of pressure from Wall Street, the board, and even your employees, be willing to stay the course. Nothing demonstrates this better than the story of Lotus Development Corporation, the company that invented the spreadsheet for the personal computer (PC).

As you remember, they were overrun by Microsoft with its version of the spreadsheet, Excel for Windows. Since Microsoft invented Windows and Lotus was late with their version of a Windows spreadsheet, Lotus was in deep trouble. Jim Manzi, the CEO at that time, decided to shift the battlefield. To him, the obvious strategy had to be *Groupware* because they had in early stages of development a product called "Lotus Notes" that was the first successful Groupware program. (Groupware is software designed for groups or networks for computers as opposed to software for individual PCs.) So Groupware became the focus at Lotus, and Jim Manzi began the process of building and supporting the Notes/Groupware business. It took an enormous effort over a five-year period but it resulted in IBM buying the company for $3.5 billion. A bold, long-term effort bailed them out of a problem that could have been fatal.

CEOs often make bad decisions that eventually lead to big trouble. They either do things that cause problems or don't do things that could have avoided problems. I once suggested to Herb Kelleher, the founder of Southwest Airlines, that he consider buying one of the shuttle airlines to obtain the New York, Washington, and Boston gates as a way to expand east. His reply was perfect, "Jack, I'd love those gates but what I don't want are their people and their airplanes." My brilliant idea would not work with Southwest's unique culture and strategy. This kind of expansion was the obvious thing *not* to do.

When danger looms, the CEO is probably the only person who can effectively take the company out of harm's way. He or she is indeed the captain of the ship—which is why every CEO should have a plaque on the wall that simply reads: **Remember the Titanic.**

Marketing's Big Problem: Wall Street

The only thing that's obvious to Wall Street is money.

Alas, poor Krispy Kreme—it had a meteoric rise and an ignominious crash. The reports stated that it was caused by "egregious" accounting to satisfy Wall Street's hunger for growth. The company became a poster child for what can happen to a brand that is being driven by the stock price instead of the marketplace.

Here's the problem: Wall Street often creates an environment that encourages bad, sometimes irrevocable, things to happen. In a way, they set up a greenhouse for trouble and, like a greenhouse, what it's all about is encouraging things to grow. The well-known economist Milton Friedman put it perfectly when he said, "We don't have a desperate need to grow. We have a desperate desire to grow." That desire for growth is at the heart of what can go wrong for many companies. Growth is the by-product of doing things right. But in itself, it is not a worthy goal.

CEOs pursue growth to ensure their tenures and to increase their take-home pay. Wall Street brokers pursue growth to ensure their reputations and to increase their take-home pay.

But is it all necessary? Not really. When you consider that people do damaging things to force unnecessary growth, you can say that it's a crime against the brand. The following true story illustrates how the desire for growth is at the root of evil doings.

I was brought in to evaluate business plans for a large multi-brand drug company. The brand managers in turn presented their next year's plans. In the course of a presentation, a young executive warned of aggressive new competition in his category that would definitely change the balance of power. But when it came to a sales projection, there was a predicted 15 percent increase. I questioned how this could be with the new competition.

His answer was they were going to do some short-term maneuvering and line extension. "Long-term, wouldn't this hurt the brand?" I asked. "Well, yes," he admitted. Then why do it? Because his boss made him put in the increase, and I would have to talk with his boss to get further clarification.

One week later, his boss admitted there was a problem but said *his* boss needed the increase because of, you guessed it, Wall Street.

Consider the saga of McDonald's. Not too many years ago their sales and earnings were flat. So the then-CEO Jack Greenberg did what most red-blooded CEOs would do: He rolled out something called a New Tastes Menu—a complex collection of 44 items to be rotated by franchisees. All this did was to slow down operations and produce lines at the cash registers. Fast food became slow food with the ensuing complaints.

All that was turned around with the late CEO Jim Cantalupo's "back to the obvious" campaign. He got off the Wall Street growth bandwagon and drove home the need for quality, cleanliness, and upgrading products and services. As he said, "We've taken our eyes off the fries." McDonald's newfound success wasn't so much about "I'm loving it"—it was more about "I'm fixing it."

Did you ever wonder why those very successful privately held companies such as Milliken or Gore-Tex rarely show up in the press? That's because no one is staring at their numbers quarter after quarter. All they have to worry about is their business. And if they are happy with it, that's all that matters. It reminds me of yet another story.

The Tico Fisherman and the Wall Street Analyst

An American businessman was at the pier of a small coastal Costa Rican village when a small boat with just one fisherman docked. Inside the small boat were several large yellow fin tuna.

The American complimented the Tico fisherman on the quality of his fish and asked how long it took to catch them.

The Tico replied, "Only a little while." The American then asked why he didn't stay out longer and catch more fish. The Tico fisherman said he had enough to support his family's immediate needs.

The American then asked, "But what do you do with the rest of your time?"

The Tico fisherman said, "I sleep late, fish a little, play with my children, take siesta with my wife Maria, stroll into the village each evening where I sip wine and play guitar with my amigos. I have a full and busy life, señor."

The American scoffed, "I am a Wall Street executive and can help you. You should spend more time fishing and with the proceeds buy a bigger boat and a Web presence. A scalable go-forward plan would provide capital for several new boats. Eventually, you would have a fleet of fishing boats. Instead of selling your catch to a middleman, you would sell directly to the processor, eventually opening your own cannery. You would control the product, processing, and distribution. You would need to leave this small coastal fishing village and move to San Jose, Costa Rica, then Los Angeles, and eventually New York City, where you would outsource tasks to third-party clients to help run your expanding enterprise in a vertical market."

The Tico fisherman asked, "But señor, how long will this all take?"

The American replied, "15 to 20 years."

"But what then, señor?"

The American laughed and said, "That's the best part. When the time is right, you will announce an IPO and sell your company stock to the public and become very rich. You will make millions."

"Millions, señor? Then what?"

The American said, "Then you will retire, move to a small coastal fishing village where you can sleep late, fish a little, play with your kids, take siesta with your wife, and stroll to the village in the evenings where you will sip wine and play your guitar with your amigos."

Moral: If you have a good business, don't try to grow it merely for the sake of growth.

No Time to Think

This section could be titled, "A tale of three meetings." It's a sad story about today's state of affairs. It's also a story that no one writes about and they should.

The first meeting took place a while ago at Intel. I was there to discuss strategy with a conference room full of mid-level executives. As the meeting began, everyone put an electronic gadget, a handheld personal organizer, on the table. What ensued could only be described as gadget envy as everyone began to comment on each other's gadgets. At this point, I broke in and asked them what they did with their gadgets. Since I was without one, I felt I must be missing something.

After they described all their gadget activities, I commented that everything they mentioned, my assistant Ann did for me. My question was, "Why are you wasting your time on an assistant's activities?" Embarrassed, they acknowledged my point, but explained the Anns were all gone at Intel—with one exception. The then CEO, Andy Grove, had three such assistants. The collective problem of the mid-level executives: They had no time to think.

Flash forward to a meeting I had with Nancy Pelosi, the speaker of the U.S. House of Representatives. It was about strategy for the 2006 elections. Hers was not a gadget problem; it was the constant flow of assistants who passed notes to her even when she was speaking. And when that stopped, most free time was dedicated to raising money. She had no time to think.

There, in two meetings, is the tragedy of our times. With the business and political worlds getting more complex and difficult, people, cell phones, BlackBerrys, or just too much communication, having quiet time to sort things out and figure out what to do, is fast disappearing. Finding the obvious requires time to think.

We have become a world of reactors, not thinkers, at a time when good thinking is so desperately needed. In business, it's rapidly segmenting markets, or rushing competition, and new technologies. In government, it's rapidly segmenting countries, changing demographics, and new disputes. In both cases, making bad decisions will cost as never before.

So what's to be done? First of all, we all have to recognize this problem. Businesspeople have to understand they are addicted to their gadgets. Politicians have to understand they are addicted to raising money. Both groups have to force themselves to take more time to think.

Then, people have to work hard not to let themselves get overwhelmed with information, much of which is of little use in making important decisions. Ignore it. Don't read it. Don't listen to it.

The best weapon we all have against too much information is our common sense. Trust it and use it. If you follow this advice, you'll find that solving the problems will get easier. This will give you more time to think about how to sell the solutions to whomever. Selling is the tough part that will take a great deal of time and energy. For here you are in the land of ego, previous bad decisions, and people with agendas. But if you're confident in your own obvious solutions, and you present your case very carefully, you have a big advantage.

With that in mind, let me end with one more meeting story. This goes back to my early days at General Electric. I was in a conference room with a crusty old marketing manager to whom I was describing a strategy to sell more electric motors. He was not looking at my flip chart. He was looking out the window. Suddenly, he noticed my discomfort. He said, "Kid, put that presentation away. Our problem isn't out there in the market. It's here in this building. Show me a presentation that can get every son of a bitch in this building pointed in the same direction, and we can flatten anything out there." It's a lesson I never forgot.

But beware, to figure out what is the obvious thing to do and how to sell the solution, you'll have to have some time to think. You'll have to fight off the distractions and all the information you don't really need. All I can wish you is good luck.

Research Can Obscure the Obvious

One of the pitfalls of the multibillion dollar marketing research industry is that researchers don't get paid for simplicity. Instead, they seem to get paid by the pound. Another true story may be in order.

I was in the office of a brand manager at Procter & Gamble. The problem was what to do with one of their largest brands. I asked a simple question about the availability of their research. I was surprised by the answer: "Research? We've got a computer full of it. How do you want it? In fact, we've got so much of it that we don't know what to do with it."

A flood of data should never be allowed to wash away your common sense and your own feeling for the market. You'll never see that obvious solution.

It's worth reviewing what this flood is washing ashore. I checked in with Robert Passikoff of BrandKeys, my favorite research company. Here are some of his and my observations:

- Customer awareness of a brand or product does not link to real customer behavior. Nor does it reinforce (or create) brand differentiation. In fact, although the phrase, "That's nothing that a whole lot of awareness won't cure" has become something of a research industry joke, those studies keep getting done. Note to everyone: *Everybody* is *aware* of GM and nobody is buying their cars.

- Segmentation studies help you identify market segments, but are they segments you really want? Or need? Or can actually market to? Often these studies end up identifying segments that you can't actually reach via any known media. But there they are. And then there's the problem of changing your strategy to appeal to different segments.

When you become everything for everybody, you become nothing in the customer's mind.

- Cross-tabulations allow you to slice-'n-dice data to your heart's content, but to what end, and to what sample sizes? Lots of data, but no insights or real differentiation.

- Customer satisfaction studies only tell you what happened the last time and nothing about what's going to happen the next. They tell you virtually nothing about the brand, and anyway, today if you can't satisfy the customer, you're not going to be in business very long.

- Visual ethnology has become hot recently. It literally means a "portrait of a people." Researchers follow consumers around to see how they interact with the product. Somehow, how they relate to a product is going to tell you how to differentiate the brand. Here interpretation rears its ugly head. Results differ from one observer to another and what is produced is open to multiple interpretations that are consistent with multiple—and inconsistent—personal points of view.

- The latest research flavor-of-the-week seems to be using neuroscience to measure brands and advertising and messaging. It's based on a body of research into how the human brain processes stimuli like ads. And if you are hooked up to a machine that's a cross between an EEG and an electric chair, researchers are able to track millisecond-by-millisecond brain responses to messaging. Nothing invasive, distracting, or out of the ordinary there! And again, it's after the fact.

- Finally, one of my favorite examples of silliness is the galvanic skin response test. You can actually wear a shirt that monitors the electric current that runs over your skin surface. When you are "aroused" by an ad or a product, the researcher "sees" your galvanic skin levels go up.

Researchers may promise to reveal attitudes, but attitudes aren't a reliable prediction of behavior. People often talk one way, but act another. Mark Twain nailed it when he observed: "You can't get the truth out of someone until they are dead and dead a long time." What you really want to get is a quick snapshot of the perceptions that exist in the mind. Not deep thoughts, not suggestions. What you're after are the perceptual strengths and weaknesses of your competitors, as they exist in the minds of the target group of consumers.

And since the ultimate marketing battle takes place in the mind, you need no more or no less. Most everything else will only confuse you.

CHAPTER 3

The Internet Can Be an Obvious Problem

Nothing in the marketing and business world has received so much hype. But be careful, it is not the ultimate solution. It's about new ways to reach people with your obvious idea. It's just another tool but it can confuse things.

Info–Clutter

The search for the obvious requires clarity of thinking. But in today's connected world, it is increasingly difficult to think clearly.

Consider what William James, a renowned psychologist and philosopher, had to say on the subject: "The art of being wise is the art of knowing what to overlook."

Business complexity is fed by the ever-increasing amount of information that is being piped into the business world in as many ways as Silicon Valley can invent. There's no escaping what David Shenk described in his book *Data Smog*, the "noxious muck and druck of the information age."

Currently, information processing accounts for half the gross national product. A lot of it ends up on paper that someone has to read. It isn't helping matters. The following statistic might threaten you, but today business managers are expected to read one million words per week. (Can you afford the time to read this?)

Peter Drucker agrees. "Computers," he says, "may have done more harm than good by making managers even more inwardly focused. Executives are so enchanted by the internal data the computer generates—and that's all it generates so far, by and large—they have neither the mind nor the time for the outside. Yet results are only on the outside. I find more and more executives less and less well informed (about the outside world)."

In support of Drucker's observation, a study in Australia indicated that the human mind can only process four variables at a time. Once this number is exceeded, the mind goes into "tilt" and we have to begin again. Today's high-tech communication tends to generate more variables than we can handle.

It's no wonder that *USA Today* did an article titled "Boomer Brain Meltdown" that described how this generation faces more frequent memory lapses. According to this article, some believe that it's not age that is the main cause of memory loss. It's information overload. Their premise is that our minds are like a computer's memory and our disks are full.

Consider numbers. In the past, all you needed to remember were your telephone number and your address. Today, it's burglar alarm codes, a social security number, e-mail numbers, fax numbers, calling card numbers, and PINs for ATMs. The digits are crowding out the words.

Some people even believe that information overload will become a medical problem. Len Riggio, CEO of Barnes & Noble, predicts that in the twenty-first century, people will be popping pills to help empty their minds. "Losing thoughts and forgetting will be the equivalent of shedding pounds and dieting," says Riggio.

I have some less drastic suggestions to reduce information right now, if you want your mind to operate at maximum efficiency and speed. Here's how to fight through the fog while still trying to see what's happening.

The first challenge is to acknowledge that you can't absorb everything you think you need to know.

Once you master that mental hurdle, things get easier. You'll be able to prioritize, delegate, and just let things slide. (You don't have to answer or even read everything that comes to you.) The very idea of actively eliminating information is a taboo for some. But what sounds like censorship is, in fact, self-preservation.

As you limit content, you'll learn to savor it more. Be ruthless as you hack your way through all the noise. Clear the decks for the important stuff.

Get started by spending two hours deciding what sources of information and intelligence are critical for you and your business:

What newsletter and periodicals are "must" reads?

What distribution lists must your name be on?

What web sites must be bookmarked?

What associations must you belong to?

Boil it all down to the highest-quality stuff and read that first. Cancel or get rid of what's only marginal.

And when you're the one doing the communicating, be more economical in everything you write, publish, broadcast, or post online.

You're supposed to be a decision maker, not an information expert. If you're blessed with an assistant, have him or her select and highlight the stuff you need to see from news magazines or survey journals in your field that abstract stories and articles. This will help you cut through all the blather.

If you can't get a story synopsis, start with the table of contents of pertinent magazines. Scan for topics and article summaries. Decide what you want to read now, tear it out for reading later, or save.

Keep a folder of "looks interesting" or "want to read" articles or mailings. They're good for plane rides.

Beware of E-Mail

E-mail's greatest virtues are that it's cheap and fast. Those also are its biggest dangers.

You are probably getting hundreds of e-mails a day from your staff, your friends, your relatives, your business contacts, your suppliers, your clients.

Then you get a BlackBerry or iPhone so that these simple e-mails can follow you wherever you travel. You will have to learn how to use your thumbs to type and sooner or later you will become addicted to that little black box. You are on your own way to what Jeffrey Haas called "Info-mania," a disease that can drain our brains.

He writes about a British study that observed that excessive day-to-day use of technology like cell phones, e-mail, and instant messaging can be more distracting and harmful to your mental acuity than smoking pot.

The Institute of Psychiatry at the University of London conducted clinical trials with volunteer office workers to measure how a constant flow of messages and information affects a person's ability to focus on problem-solving tasks.

Participants were asked first to work in a quiet environment and then to work while being inundated with e-mail, instant messaging, and phone calls. Although they were told not to respond to messages, researchers found their subjects' attention was significantly disturbed.

Instead of boosting productivity, the constant data stream seriously reduced their ability to focus. The study reported that an average worker's functioning IQ falls 10 points when distracted by ringing telephones and incoming e-mails, more than twice the four-point drop seen following a 2002 Carleton University study on the impact of smoking marijuana.

Too much data clamors for conscious attention. It all wants to evolve into information and then knowledge. Just deciding what to ignore takes intellectual effort, and, inevitably, the quality of work suffers.

The quality of life suffers, too.

The study showed that 62 percent of adults are literally addicted to checking e-mail and text messages during meetings, in the evening, and on weekends.

Half of workers respond to e-mails immediately or within 60 minutes, and one in five people are happy to interrupt a business or social meeting to respond to an e-mail or telephone message within 60 minutes.

The study warns of the abuse of always-on technology and calls this endemic condition *info-mania*. If you sense you have early indications of this disease, here are some tips:

- Decide whether you'll actually open and read e-mail by what's in the header. Scan by sender and subject. Give messages from your clients and the boss priority.

- Look for filters in your e-mail program. Filters let you prioritize messages from key people and separate them from other stuff.

- Lighten up your load in the first place. Don't put your e-mail address on your business cards. Give it only to people who need it.

- Open e-mail only at set times—perhaps when you start work or at the end of the day. The whole point of e-mail is that the other person doesn't know when or even if you looked at it. If your computer constantly flags incoming mail, and if you constantly reply, the little buggers just multiply.

- Send brief responses. Discourage people from writing long e-mails or leaving long voice mails.

- Unless you're retired, ask friends not to forward trivia, chatter, jokes, and other junk.

If you just need to get facts straight or solicit opinions, use e-mail or fax. But if a subject needs some discussion, don't use e-mail. Pick up the phone or walk down the hall to discuss it.

And don't be seduced by the endless array of new gadgets being offered that do everything imaginable.

Does all this gear make life simpler? Make the executive more productive? More efficient? Are you kidding! Professor Hugh Heclo of George Mason University observes: "In the long run, excesses of technology means that the comparative advantage shifts from those with information glut to those with ordered knowledge, from those who can process vast amounts of throughput to those who can explain what is worth knowing, and why."

So as you fight through the smog, remember:

- There is a difference between data and information.
- You can get addicted to your favorite communications device.
- Don't be a pack rat. You can retrieve anything electronically.
- Most requests are not as urgent as the sender believes.
- Always separate urgent messages from nonurgent ones.
- Always respond briefly and to the point. Don't add more noise than signal.

Is Word-of-Mouth Marketing All It's Cracked Up to Be?

Suddenly, everyone is talking about word-of-mouth marketing. You can tell things are getting a little out of hand when you discover there is now a Word-of-Mouth Marketing Association or WOMMA. And there are conferences popping up all over the world on this subject. One conference had over 400 attendees.

And that's not all. Now we have a new dictionary to learn. Word-of-mouth is now buzz marketing, viral marketing, community marketing, grass-roots marketing, evangelist marketing, product seeding, influencer marketing, cause marketing, conversation creation, brand blogging, and referral programs. That's the good stuff. What's not so good is stealth marketing, shilling, infiltration, comment spam, defacement, and falsifications.

If you're like me, you're probably a little confused about all this so let's put some things into perspective.

First of all, word-of-mouth is no new thing in marketing, much less "the next big thing" that WOMMA declares. Having a third-party endorsement of your product has always been the Holy Grail. It makes your product more believable. In prior days, we used to try and find the "early adapters" for a product. We figured they had big mouths and loved to tell their friends and neighbors about their new widget.

What's different today is people have many more ways to communicate. Instead of just verbal, we now have digital communications. Online chatter far surpasses over-the-fence chatter in every way with the exception of clearly knowing the person with whom you are chattering. The trouble is that the ease of communicating en masse has raised the noise level to mind-boggling levels. That's the good news.

Now for the bad news: How many people really want to chatter about products? Do you really want to talk about your toothpaste or your toilet paper? Even people with prestige products tend not to chatter about them. All you really want is to be seen driving up in one. If it's a Harley Davidson motorcycle, you're part of a club and that's all they talk about. But they don't need buzz.

No product got as much buzz and public relations as the Segway gyroscopic scooter. The problem is that most of the buzz was negative. "Funny looking or dangerous on sidewalks" is not what you want to hear. Buzz can kill you if you don't have the right product.

The very expensive remake movie *King Kong* was a bust because of a lot of negative word-of-mouth. "Too long, too loud, and overdone." The Pontiac G6 giveaway on *Oprah* got a lot of buzz but the car died at the box office. People would take one for free but not if they had to pay for it. You've got to have a product or service people want to talk about in a positive way and there aren't many of these around.

But now for the really bad news: How do you get people to say the right thing or talk about your obvious idea? There's no way to control that word-of-mouth. Do I want to give up control and let consumers take over my campaign? No way. They aren't getting paid based on how many widgets get sold. If I go to all this trouble developing a positioning strategy for my product, I want to see that message delivered. Buzz can get your name mentioned, but you can't depend on much else. Not too many celebrities or "mouths" will do a stand up commercial about your product versus its competitor. Nor will they check with you in advance on what to say.

This all brings me to my word-of-mouth on word-of-mouth marketing. It's not the next big thing. It's just another tool in your arsenal. If you have a way to get your strategy or point of difference talked about by your customers and prospects, that's terrific. It will help but you're going to have to surround it with a lot of other effort, including, if you'll pardon the expression, advertising. You just can't buy mouths the way you can buy media. And mouths can stop talking about you in a heartbeat once something else comes along to talk about.

What caught my eye was a newspaper report of a very insightful interview with an advertising agency about just such a story from the marketing world. All the right questions were asked about Smirnoff trying to generate some buzz for a new iced tea malt beverage. Here are the questions, the answers, and my observations about the agency's answers.

Q. Why did this program appear only online?

A. The client didn't have a lot of money.

Observation: Seagram is a rich company. If iced tea with Smirnoff is a big idea, why not spend enough to introduce it properly? My ex-partner Al Ries and I wrote a book titled *The 22 Immutable Laws of Marketing.* The 22nd law was called the Law of Resources: Without proper resources, even the best ideas will not get off the ground. It looks like they are violating this law.

Q. The first time I watched the video, I didn't know it was for Smirnoff Ice Tea. Why so little appearance of the brand name and the product?

A. We can't play by the rules of advertising because if people see the product too much, they will reject it.

Observation: That's a big problem. Introducing a new product that's barely visible and easily missed isn't going to get the job done.

Q. So lack of branding is supposed to make people think it's not an ad?

A. It's just that it doesn't feel like an ad. They see it as fun.

Observation: Are you entertaining people and having fun or are you trying to sell something? Without a reason to buy a product, you won't have many people, beyond the curious, who will buy it.

Q. How did the lack of the Smirnoff name play with the client?

A. They bought into it. They understand that advertising is no longer talking at someone. It's about engaging with the consumer. You have to be more entertaining.

> Brands aren't advertisers anymore. They are something consumers get involved with and take part in.
>
> *Observation:* That pretty much answers my earlier questions. This agency sees itself in the entertainment business, not the selling business. Hollywood has come to Madison Avenue. If that's the case, I can only add the famous Edward R. Murrow line, "Goodnight and good luck."

Once again, it's important to understand that all these new ways to reach consumers are just new tools. You still have to have search for *the obvious:* the right product, the right strategy, and the right differentiating idea in relation to your competition.

Sure you might get some exposure and even a few buyers for less money on the Internet. But, as they say, you get what you pay for. That famous online Burger King subservient chicken generated a lot of buzz and a lot of clicks but not much business. What generated business was pushing The Whopper. Now there's the obvious beef.

Consider the release of the movie *Snakes on a Plane*. It boasted vigorous marketing on the Internet. The strategy was designed to drive fans into theaters at a time that movies were working hard to hold their own against other forms of entertainment. The results were big expectations because of extensive buzz but not much business. Some experts suggested that the most entertaining part of the experience was talking about the movie on the Internet, not going to the film. Besides, if you're online a lot, who has time to go to the movies? Internet buzz doesn't always translate into sales. And never forget that the purpose of a business is to generate customers—not laughs or fun or involvement.

My view? How many people want to see a movie about snakes on a plane? Only those horror film addicts that love that kind of stuff. As for the mainstream audience, a lousy idea is a lousy idea no matter how much buzz it receives. In this case, you didn't have an obvious strategy but an obvious problem. But, hey, I could be wrong. Pontiac spent all its marketing dollars to introduce its G5 coupe online. They admit that it certainly won't generate as much awareness as traditional media but they will reach their target of younger men.

Reaching them is one thing. Selling them is another. It will be interesting to see how it all works out. Using the Internet to keep in touch with customers makes sense as does using it along with traditional media. To me, using it exclusively to launch a new product is pushing the envelope.

Into the Abyss

The Association of National Advertisers held their annual conference recently. Speaker after speaker addressed the growing popularity of what is known as *behavioral targeting* as opposed to basing pitches on consumer attitudes, opinions, or perceptions.

The ability of the Internet to monitor what consumers are doing by tracking what web sites they visit is fueling interest in what many call understanding our customer better. (I call it getting totally confused by your customers.) The result, according to one speaker, will be different messages in different media for different customers. While admitting it will be terribly complex, they feel that this is the way it will be. I say many will be led by all this into the abyss of blurred brands and hopeless confusion from which they may never recover. This is no way to find the obvious.

Anheuser-Busch dived in by studying "use occasions." Then they launched an ambitious online project that offered entertainment programming named Bud TV. It turned out to be a bust so the "content is being rethought." But here's my favorite line from their presentation. "The programming had nothing to do with our brands." I say, then, what's the purpose of all this money and effort?

While these marketing folks are trying to figure out how to be everything for everybody, category after category is sliding into commoditization. As I mentioned earlier, while working on the updated revision of my book *Differentiate or Die*, I came across some extensive research on this subject conducted by the research company Brand Keys. Here are the highlights:

- Degree of differentiation differed by category. In the Bar Soap category, for example, 100 percent of the brands differentiated themselves. Fifty percent (50 percent) of Credit Card offerings were found to stand for something in the minds of the consumers. But Banks, Motor Oil, and 20 other categories—nearly a third of all the categories examined—did not have any differentiated brands. The products and services were known, but not known for anything in particular.

- To better explain this, take the category of Banks. They produce one meaningless slogan after another. How about these: "Where money lives." Or "Embracing ingenuity" or "The clean Swiss bank" or "Here today. Here tomorrow." Slogans like these and endless mergers have commoditized the category.

- On the other hand, take a category such as Automotive. This has a reasonable number at 38 percent. This means that you have a fair number of differentiated brands such as Toyota (Reliability) or BMW (Driving) or Volvo (Safety) or Mercedes (Engineering) or Ferrari (Speed). It also means that you have a large number of placeholders with little differentiation. Think General Motors or Ford.

- Of the 75 categories measured, 20 had 0 percent differentiation. Hundreds of brand names were so badly blurred as to not stand for anything different. Twenty-eight categories had less than 30 percent of the brands differentiated. In other words, two-thirds of these categories were not well differentiated or on their way to being commoditized.

So against that backdrop, you end up with advertising that isn't based on why your brand is different but how people use it at different times. Or worse than that, you just put out your brand name and let your customers figure out what it's about and when to use it while you keep track. What they perceive just isn't that important. If they think we are all similar, so be it.

Ladies and gentlemen, this is not the road to the obvious. This kind of thinking is the road to rack and ruin. Welcome to the abyss.

4

Advertising People Can Be an Obvious Problem

Unfortunately, most advertising people look for the creative, not the obvious. For them, the obvious is too simple and not clever enough. The old guard—Leo Burnett, David Ogilvy, and Bill Bernbach—understood this. The new guard, whomever they are, don't.

Advertising as Theatre

Over the years, I've raised some questions about Super Bowl advertising and how it lacked any selling messages—which is especially wasteful at $2.7 million for a 30-second spot.

Most advertisers and their agencies are creating advertising designed to entertain, not to sell. You could say they are all on the same wasteful page. They are all a little crazy. It's all about getting laughs or generating shock value. It's about theater, not marketing.

People will instantly jump up at my observations and say that I'm old-fashioned. Their defense will be that if you love their commercial, you will love their product and you will buy it. Well, dear readers, history has pretty much declared that premise as wrong.

Consider the beer business. No one has poured as much money into Super Bowl ads as Anheuser-Busch. Over the years, we've seen Clydesdales playing football, frogs talking, funny gag after funny gag. The latest features a Clydesdale working out so as to join the team. Has it helped sell beer? Not that I can see; the beer business has been flat and declining for years. The only ones making gains are the imports (Corona) or the specialty beers (Sam Adams and company). None of these were Super Bowl advertisers.

The colas have also poured millions into the big game. Has it helped sell colas? Not that I can see; the cola category has been flat and declining in recent years. The big gains have been made by sports drinks (Gatorade), water, and specialty drinks. None of these were Super Bowl advertisers.

Rather than pick on different commercials, let me make some observations on what is going on here.

First of all, you have the *media factor*. All the media has piled on to write endlessly about all these commercials. They write as if they are reviewing movies or plays. Was it funny? Did it offend someone? Did their readers like it? Never a question about whether it offered a reason to buy the product. The ones that did just that are declared boring. So what's an agency to do to get critical acclaim? You bet, get wild and crazy.

Next we have the *buzz factor*. With the arrival of the Internet, everyone wants to see his commercial talked about as it lives on in his Web-based campaigns. But what are people talking about? Not the product or why it's different. They are talking about the gag. I read one columnist's comment that these Web visits are the "beginning of the selling process." If there's no selling message in the commercial, what process is he talking about? What's the purpose of people looking at a bad commercial online? This kind of thinking will inevitably lead to top management beginning to question whether all this hoopla results in selling more products. The obvious answer to that question could cause the advertising industry some long-term problems.

Finally, let me tell you a true story about the importance of a consumer liking or disliking your advertising. It gets to the essence of the rationale for all this "theater." Over the years, I've been invited in as an advertising expert on a number of call-in radio shows. On more than one occasion, I've been asked why some advertisers produce commercials that are not fun to watch. I reply that most "not fun" commercials that continue to run are effective in selling products or they wouldn't continue to run them.

But, then I ask some questions and usually get the exact same answers:

Question: Tell me about a commercial that you like.

The answer usually describes one with a child or a dog or some human interest.

Question: What were they advertising and who was the advertiser?

The answer usually was that they weren't sure but they did like the commercial.

Question: Tell me about a commercial that you didn't like.

The answer often describes the product, the brand, and exactly what it did. I then tell the listener that her question has been answered.

So there it is, take your pick. Run advertising that people like but don't know exactly why they should buy a product or run advertising that people don't find entertaining but know exactly why they should buy your product instead of a competitor's product.

If it was my $2.7 million, I'd pick the latter.

Loving a Brand?

In a recent *BusinessWeek*, there was a story of how Procter & Gamble is attempting to "stake out the emotional high ground" for their Tide detergent. This attempting to establish an emotional connection with your customers tends to show up more and more in agency presentations. Agency CEO Robert Kevin even wrote a book on the subject titled *Lovemarks: The Future Beyond Brands*.

I don't want to throw cold water on all this emotion and love but I have some questions about all this kind of activity.

First of all, who gets emotional about detergent, or toothpaste or, for that matter, most of the products out there? If you look at the success of Wal-Mart, you can safely say that the only thing that people really get emotional about is price.

Second, can emotion be a differentiating idea? What's to prevent a competitor from trying to be just as emotional as you are. Consider the credit card wars. Visa built their brand around the concept of "Everywhere you want to be." They took ownership of the "Everywhere" or acceptance attribute. This is the No. 1 attribute in credit cards.

MasterCard stumbled around until they landed on the emotional strategy of "For everything else, there's MasterCard." Not bad but not great. In my estimation, they should have become "Main Street's Credit Card." Give Visa the globe; you take home base. At least "everything else" plays in that direction.

The best thing that this program did was to encourage Visa to leave their brilliant strategy and get emotional. Their new strategy is "Life takes Visa." That's good news for MasterCard. And what's funny is that everyone is getting into "Life." Coke never should have left the "Real Thing." But what are they today? That's right, they want you to come to the "Coke side of life." (Maybe you should buy your Coke with a Visa card?)

But let's get back to Tide and their attempt to get emotional. My question here is, why? They have a 42 percent share of the category. They are America's No. 1 detergent (see Chapter 13, "Leadership Is a Powerful Differentiator," *Differentiate or Die,* second edition). Leadership is the obvious strategy they should employ.

Procter & Gamble is almost single-handedly "Keeping America in clean clothes." The reason for this is that Tide knows fabric best. The proof of this claim is their 42 percent share. (That's a number that will make any product manager truly emotional.)

Finally, is there a role for emotion in developing a strategy?

It depends on what emotion you are talking about. Prestige is an emotion. Why do I buy a $60,000 car? Obviously, to impress my friends and neighbors. But you still have to offer a rationale for the purchase such as its engineering or whatever.

The same goes for an expensive watch that doesn't keep time better than a Timex. The best line that Rolex ever came up with is "It takes a year to build a Rolex." I would make that the positioning strategy and never make the watch any faster.

With expensive, prestige products, the high price delivers the prestige. (How else can I impress someone?) But you still need that rationale or reason to buy for a customer to latch on to so that they can justify wasting their money.

Cosmetics are sold on the emotion of that magic in the bottle that will fight off aging or attract the opposite sex. Whole

Foods plays on the emotion of *health* with all their natural foods.

Quiksilver surfboard clothing is sold on the emotion of being cool like the bronzed surfboarders that hang out in Hawaii. In all these cases there is a different kind of product story.

But sanitary napkins or disposable diapers? Don't give me emotion, give me a reason to buy your brand instead of someone else's. And if you don't give me a reason, you better have a low price because that really gets me excited.

Interestingly, I asked a psychologist in the communications field about all this. She had an interesting observation:

> Emotion without substance is like infatuation that disappoints in the light of day. Without a real difference, an ongoing relationship with the consumer is lost.

The pushing of all this emotion stuff has become the big excuse for advertising agencies that are having problems with coming up with that reason to buy. Here's what WPP's Sir Martin Sorrell had to say:

> Differences between products and services are becoming less. Therefore, the psychological differentiation and lifestyle differentiation are more important.

To that statement, my response is to quote Pogo:

> We have met the enemy and it is us.

The Emotional Trap

It's worth spending more time on *emotion*. Let me give you two examples.

Once upon a time Continental Airlines had a simple, rational reason for you to fly with them instead of their competitors. Their slogan: "More airline for the money." They had plenty of support for this idea and they still have. Then some agency that didn't come up with that line changed it to "Work hard. Fly right." What in the world does that mean? I suspect that their argument was something about how this was a more powerful emotional argument. That's silly.

Lowe's, a very successful challenger to Home Depot, had a brilliant rational argument for shopping at their stores. Their slogan: "Improving home improvement." So what did they do? They replaced this concept with a more emotional slogan, "Let's build something together." More silliness.

This kind of advertising is being produced all over the industry as clients are being sold on the concept that people have to love brands, not just buy them. I'm not saying that you shouldn't have an artful or dramatic way to involve a prospect in your message. The current Wal-Mart advertising is a good example of this kind of work. Their advertising uses a tried and true "slice of life" commercial to dramatize the fact that the money you save will enable you to have more fun in life. Nicely done. But saving money is still the reason to shop at Wal-Mart—fun or no fun.

All advertising and marketing have to do is supply that obvious reason to buy your product instead of your competitor's product.

Interestingly, some folks are finally beginning to weigh in on the more rational approach to selling. Mark Penn, in his book called *Microtrends* makes the point that "the rational side of people is far more powerful in many areas of life than the purely emotional side." He should know because he is widely regarded as the most perceptive pollster in American politics. He is also the worldwide CEO of Burson-Marsteller, a very large public relations firm.

But what really begins to undermine this emotional silliness is an important piece of research conducted by the digital video-recorder maker TiVo Inc. They examined the commercial viewing habits of some 20,000 TiVo equipped households including which and what campaigns are fast-forwarded by the lowest percentage of viewers. All this was written about by Burt Helm in a *BusinessWeek* article titled, *"Which Ads Don't Get Skipped?"* The results, so far, weigh heavily in favor of rational arguments. Relevancy outweighs creativity in TV commercials by a lot. The ads on the "least-fast-forwarded" list aren't funny, they aren't touching, and they aren't clever.

Can you believe it? In June, the No. 1 least fast-forwarded campaign was for the home gym Bowflex. People looked at those good-looking folks on those machines and said, "Maybe I can have a body like that." That sculptured abdomen is one heck of a rationale for a machine like that. Other winners were for CORT furniture company, Dominican Republic tourism, and Hooters Restaurant. Can you imagine, several throw 800-numbers in at the end of the commercial?

The article said it all at the end when Burt Helm wrote, "If TiVo owners are any guide, it seems that just reaching the right audience and putting the product right out there sets you leagues ahead, no matter how banal or bludgeoning your spot is. So if you have only 30 seconds, why not skip this soft seduction and just sell, sell, sell?"

Runaway Sloganeering

An obvious idea is rarely a slogan. If you spend any time looking at advertising, you will be struck with the fact that the marketing world is mired in what can only be called

runaway sloganeering, which is a long way from obvious selling ideas.

If you doubt this, take the following slogan quiz. Here are
some current multimillion dollar slogans for some very big
national advertisers. See how many you name the sponsoring
company for. (The answers are at the end of this section.)

Quiz Number 1
- Your future made easier.
- Your world delivered.
- Yes you can.
- Way of light.
- Uncommon wisdom.
- Always worth it.
- Shift.
- Today's the day.
- Live richly.

I know what you're thinking. It's not fair to take a slogan
out of context. They are just some ideas for a commercial or a
print advertisement. But that's the problem. If you think like
that, you'll probably end up with a cute but meaningless set of
words. A good slogan should be a position or differentiating
idea. And none on that list come close to being that. What
you're after are the likes of what I call Hall of Fame slogans.
Here are some slogans that I suspect you'll have little trouble
naming the sponsor for:

Quiz Number 2
- Diamonds are forever.
- The real thing.

- The ultimate driving machine.
- Everywhere you want to be.
- Better ingredients. Better Pizza.
- Eat Fresh.

Some of these have been around for decades. One is remembered (even though it hasn't been used in decades). All go to the essence of the product, not to the commercial. None of them can easily be expressed by a competitor. (That is the litmus test for a slogan.) For example, Nokia has been running the meaningless slogan "Connecting People." Well, what else does a cell phone connect? That same idea could easily be expressed by Motorola or Ericsson. What really differentiates Nokia is their position of leadership. The slogan they should be running is "The world's No. 1 cell phone."

That same leadership concept would make far more sense than "I'm lovin' it" for McDonald's. When you consider their size and global reach, you could easily position them as "The world's favorite place to eat." Agency folks would quickly label leadership as boring and not interesting. And how can I put it to music?

What these folks ignore is the psychological power of leadership. People tend to buy what others buy. It's what psychologists call the "herd effect." (People judge their actions correct to the degree they see others performing them.) But instead of using this psychology, they choose to be cute and creative. Next stop, a meaningless slogan. What many agency folks and marketers fail to understand is that there are many ways to differentiate a product beyond the product itself. In addition to leadership, there are heritage, attributes, how it's made, and next generation strategies to pursue. I wrote a book on all this titled *Differentiate or Die*.

The underlying problem is that these slogans do not help or produce a reason to buy a certain product over another. And they certainly aren't obvious ideas. This means that the advertising isn't very effective. This in turn causes marketers to lose faith in advertising. The bottom line: Meaningless slogans are like a virus that is undermining the world of marketing. Unless it's stopped, we are watching category after category become commodities.

And that, dear readers, is big trouble unless you have a very low price.

Quiz Number 1 Answers
Your future made easier. **ING**
Your world delivered. **AT&T**
Yes you can. **Sprint**
Way of light. **Suzuki**
Uncommon wisdom. **Wachovia**
Always worth it. **Bud Light**
Shift. **Nissan**
Today's the day. **Monster.com**
Live richly. **Citibank**

Quiz Number 2 Answers
Diamonds are forever. **DeBeers**
The real thing. **Coke**
The ultimate driving machine. **BMW**
Everywhere you want to be. **Visa**
Better ingredients. Better Pizza. **Papa John's**
Eat Fresh. **Subway**

The Creativity Trap

At present, the advertising industry is in some disarray. People are questioning the viability of traditional advertising. Many new forms of marketing tools are being cooked up daily, most of which revolve around the digital world in which we live.

The biggest threat is TiVo and the ability to digitally record shows and skip by the commercials. All this has led the advertising industry to declare that more creativity is needed to keep people watching. Thus, emotion, humor, or whatever it takes to freeze viewers is the advertising rule of the day. As I've already noted, even a powerful idea like the Visa tag line, "Everywhere you want to be" gets changed to an emotional tag line "Life takes Visa." That's bad enough but their competitor, American Express, is running a program that says: "My life. My card."

What's going on here?

To me, it's creativity run amok. What the advertising people don't realize is that selling isn't about being creative or cute or imaginative. It's all about logic, which is a science that deals with the rules and tests of sound thinking.

A trip to a dictionary will define a logical argument as one that is cogent, compelling, convincing, valid, clear. It shows skill in thinking or reasoning. And it's also obvious.

Now doesn't that sound like an argument you would like to have to support what you're trying to sell? You'd better believe it. And yet, how many logical arguments do you come across in the marketing world? Very few. That lack of logic is at the heart of most programs that fail. However, if you can see the logic in the argument, chances are you've got a winner.

If Avis is only number 2 in rent-a-cars, then it figures that they have to try harder. It's not creative, it's logical. It's obvious.

If IBM's size covers all aspects of computing, then it's obvious that they can integrate all the pieces better than any other manufacturer. Integrated computing is what makes them different.

Consider the Swedish company SKF. For over 100 years, they have been a world leader in bearings of all kinds. One of their young executives appeared in my office asking how they could improve how they are perceived in terms of saving energy. I told him it was obvious. All they had to do was tell their story of how they "make things run better." And efficient machines use less energy than inefficient machines.

But, he reported, we are in the midst of a big advertising program about "knowledge engineering." My response was that his only obvious move was to connect "knowledge engineering" to the concept of "making things run better." In other words, this was their underlining technology. It's how they design and continue to improve their family of bearings. And better bearings are often at the core of increased performance and energy savings.

It's not all they do in this process of improving performance, but it is at the heart of SKF's 100-year history. Without bearings, the world would run very badly. With new and improved bearings, the world will run better and better and save more and more energy. Customers come to SKF to make things run better, not to acquire knowledge engineering. That's painfully obvious.

So, dear reader, how do you think he did in these efforts to change a runaway slogan? You're right. Not very well because the CEO was not involved and the person in charge of advertising had his ego on the line.

Since logic is a science, it's logical that constructing an obvious selling proposition or point of difference should be a science, not an art. And yet the creative faction fights this idea tooth and nail. They hate the thought of being locked into a process that limits their creative musing. They tend to dislike obvious ideas.

But what's worse is to see a company go through the strategy process and come up with a straightforward logical argument for their brand, then turn it over to the creative folks and watch the argument disappear in a cloud of singing and dancing or whatever.

Once, while working with a bank on their strategy, we discovered that they were the leader in Small Business Administration loans in their trading area. Most of those loans, it turned out, were going to recent immigrants starting businesses in America—people pursuing the American dream of success.

The recommended strategy was logical and direct. What made this bank different was that it was "the home of the American dream."

Everyone liked the idea, and it was handed over to an agency for implementation. When we saw it again it had become: "We bank on your dreams."

So much for their obvious differentiating idea.

I'm not naïve about why agencies like to push creativity. They see all those award shows about creativity as their ticket to more new business. The problem is that these activities only lead to more wild and crazy advertising that lacks a clear reason to buy. Nobody gives out awards for clear logic. All this has to stop if the agency business is to regain their footing.

What's to be done? Well, I suggest that advertising agencies do away with their creative departments and replace them with dramatizing departments. In other words, replace creativity with dramativity.

The fact is that creativity was always a misnomer. An agency isn't creating something. The company or product or service already exists. What they are doing is figuring out what is the best way to sell it. That, simply stated, means to take that logical, differentiating argument and dramatize it.

How do you make that argument exciting and involving? Long ago, Crest toothpaste in a TV commercial declared, "Triumph over tooth decay." Volvo put a car next to a tank in a print advertisement with the headline: "The execution is different but the concept is basically the same." How's that for dramatizing a safety strategy?

The new retro Alka Seltzer ads are wonderful dramatizations of solving the problem of overeating. Today, you see some animals introducing some offbeat drama as they deliver a pretty good message. The Geico Gekko and the Aflac Duck are pretty good examples though you have to be careful about stuff like this because it can be visually distracting. And when this happens, people stop listening and no selling message is delivered.

However you choose to introduce dramativity into your advertising, one thing is clear: Your reason to buy must be perfectly logical and obvious and not submerged into what people call creativity.

Sometimes I wonder if the advertising industry has lost touch with the meaning of advertising. If you look at a dictionary, the definition is, "To call public attention to, especially in order to sell." So, there it is, the role of advertising is not to entertain, it's to sell. And don't fall prey to the argument that people won't pay attention unless you entertain them. If you have an interesting piece of news or a pretty good reason to buy, you can get people to stop and listen to what you have to say.

Want an example of how to do it? Start your next commercial with a person looking into the camera and saying, "Before you zap me, hang on for a bit. I have some important news to tell you about."

You'll freeze everyone in their seats and get their undivided attention. Then you'll get a chance to sell them, not just entertain them.

The press is abuzz with stories about big companies moving dollars out of traditional advertising media and into product placements and other newer marketing methods. One expert after another is predicting that the ad industry, as we know it, has lost its way and is in decline. Stories about TiVo, buzz, and the Internet are all the vogue. Before everyone packs up their resumes and jumps ship, I think it's time for a more reasoned view of things or one that gets us away from all the negative hype and the doom and gloom. Let's start with what should be the obvious role of the advertising agency.

Traditionally, the agency's role is to be the objective outsider. Their role is to counsel the client on how to best sell their products or services to their marketplace—how to position the brand in relation to the competition. And how to verbalize their message with that "reason to buy." Candor and honesty were always the hallmarks of a good agency/client relationship because agencies played a major role in developing strategy for their clients.

A true story is in order here. Many years ago, a senior account supervisor was reminiscing to me about the old days in the business. He recounted a meeting in a hotel where the CEO of the client and the head of the agency were lying in bed together discussing strategy. He said, "Jack, the industry problem is that we're not in bed with the CEOs anymore."

He was right. As the years have rolled by, I've seen less and less of that kind of relationship. Agencies have backed off on pushing strategy as clients became more assertive in this regard. Instead, agencies retreated to creativity, emotion, or humor as their contributions to the brand. The net result: Today a lot of advertising lacks that reason to buy. Too many people looked at the advertisement and said, "What are they trying to sell?" It's no wonder clients are beginning to question traditional advertising's usefulness.

How to Fix the Ad Industry

Step 1: Get Back to Strategy

Forget about emotion, bonding, borrowed interest, or show business. Agencies have to rebuild their reputations around being able to help top management figure out the right competitive strategy for a brand. In simple terms, they have to be able to help establish the point of difference for a brand. Forty years ago, it was called a *unique selling proposition*. In more recent years, it was called a *position*. In all cases, it's why a customer should prefer your product over the many other choices out there.

This difference is your ultimate weapon against all this talk about who needs advertising when you have "buzz" and "product placement." Unfortunately, most of these new marketing tools that are getting all the attention don't enable you to deliver that message. All they are good for is getting a name out there with no story attached to it.

Consider again the famous *Oprah* Pontiac giveaway of 200 Pontiac G6s. (It won a Cannes Media Lion.) The result was great press but lousy sales, 30 percent below expectations. What was missing was the story about why I should buy one if I didn't get one for free. Strategy gives you a guide for all these newfangled activities. The differentiating idea can be carefully introduced into these nonadvertising vehicles. In other words, your carefully developed strategy is the cornerstone for your multimedia plans. They can extend your selling message beyond advertising.

Step 2: Dramatize the Strategy

Creative people tend to resist a strategic approach to advertising. To them, it restricts their creativity. They sometimes view advertising as an art form. To me, the role of a good creative person is to take the strategy and dramatize it in a way that better involves the prospects. In a way, you are dramatizing the reason to buy. It could be a product demonstration or a dramatic solution to a perceived problem. Whatever it is, it captures people's attention while you deliver your sales message.

Consider BMW as a model client. Over 20 years and many agencies ago, they launched an attack on Mercedes with the dramatic concept of: "The ultimate sitting machine versus the ultimate driving machine." Today they are still driving with the same concept and are one of the world's most successful car companies. Great strategies never die. Nor do they fade away.

Step 3: Do Away with Awards

Do away with all those creativity awards shows á la Cannes and Clios. Nothing does more long-term damage to the industry than making creative folks think that they are making movies rather than commercials. Consider the "Curse of the Clio." It's widely known that a large number of Clio winners lost their accounts not too long after taking home their statuettes. All this undermines the industry's perceptions of being strategic in its work. It would be like lawyers getting awards for creativity in trials. Agencies are supposed to be professionals helping clients solve problems and sell products. Their award should be getting to keep the account.

Besides, clients are on to the fact that awards are there to help agencies get more accounts, not for helping clients get more business. That is not a very helpful perception for an industry under attack.

CHAPTER
5

Marketing People Can Be an Obvious Problem

Marketing people often don't appreciate what they should be focusing on. Most get hopelessly entangled in corporate egos and complicated projects. It's no wonder that the job tenure of a chief marketing officer is less than two years.

The Tinkering Factor

The *Wall Street Journal* reported that Peter Brabeck, the departing CEO of Nestlé, put the company on a diet.

He discovered that the food maker was churning out 130,000 variations of its brands and 30 percent weren't making any money. He launched an aggressive plan to jettison weaker brands and simplify the organization. It's bye-bye to low-carb Kit-Kats and lemon cheesecake-flavored chocolate. (Can you imagine?)

Nestlé faces a predicament that haunts many companies that have acquired other companies to a point that these companies are almost impossible to manage. When you're into dog food, chocolate, baby food, ice cream, coffee, and on and on, you can easily see the problem.

But what's even worse is that these megacompanies end up with hundreds of marketing people sitting around cooking up new ideas that aren't very good ideas. Or they sit around and try to figure out how to improve things. They just can't stop tinkering. It's an obvious problem. What top management fails to understand is that the road to chaos is paved with improvements.

In all my years in the business, I've never seen a marketing person come into a new assignment, look around, and say, "Things look pretty good. Let's not touch a thing."

To the contrary, all red-blooded marketing people want to get in there and start improving things. They want to make their mark. Just *sitting there* wouldn't feel right.

When a company has offices full of marketing people, you've got to expect endless tinkering with a brand. It's how they keep from getting bored.

Someone on the Prell Shampoo brand says, "Hey, why don't we add a blue Prell to our line of green Prell?" Of course, this ignores the consumer perception that if it isn't green, it can't be Prell.

Bad idea.

At McDonald's someone says, "Hey, let's take advantage of the pizza trend and add McPizza to the menu!" Of course, this ignores the consumer perception that hamburger joints can't know much about making pizza.

Bad idea.

Someone at Anheuser-Busch says, "Hey, why don't we add dry and ice beers to our lineup?" Of course, this ignores the consumer perception that beer is usually wet and not served over ice.

Bad idea.

Someone at Volkswagen says, "Let's introduce a $60,000 automobile called the Phaeton." Of course, this ignores the fact that in America a Volkswagen has no prestige as a brand.

Bad idea.

At BIC, the marketing people, because Mr. Bic is still around, are busy putting the brand on everything they can think of such as pens, lighters, razor blades, pantyhose, perfume, and even sailboards.

Bad idea.

Someone at Heinz, the king of ketchup, decided that they should also make mustard. And, to save money, let's use the same shaped bottles. People thought it was yellow ketchup.

Bad idea.

Someone at Daimler Benz figured out that luxury cars aren't enough. Buying Chrysler would give them a wide range of vehicles to sell everywhere.

Very bad idea.

And, of course, you can't leave out the endless and painfully expensive tinkering with logos. Xerox, with one of the great logo designs of all time, decided to change it and have the big letter "X" break up in pieces to signify going digital. This was unfortunately at about the same time the company ran into serious financial problems. All the new logo said to people was that Xerox was disintegrating.

Luckily, a new CEO and smarter heads prevailed and they went back to the original logo. But now they are at it again. They have changed it to lower case and added a ball logo à la AT&T. They can't stop tinkering.

The obvious has to line up with the perceptions in the customer's mind, not go against them. What people inside the company perceive as improvements often cause confusion inside the mind of the prospect.

Once you've gotten a brand up to altitude, your watchword should be "steady as she goes." A brand can only stand for one thing in the mind and the more things you try to make it stand for, the more the mind loses focus on what it is. Endless variations give marketing people something to do while they do long-term damage to a brand or a company.

When it comes to promoting tourism, nothing comes close to endlessly tinkering or changing a successful program. Why? Because of politics. New administrations come into power and they quickly want their own programs. Such was the case of New Zealand. Their latest slogan promotes New Zealand as "the youngest country on earth." Now, there is a silly idea when you consider that people want to see the old, not the new.

Some years ago, I was asked about how to position New Zealand. I pointed out that it was painfully obvious. What they had in spades was incredible physical beauty. Anyone that's been there will say that it is a "beautiful country." So, since they had two islands, the way to dramatize this was to raise the question of what island was most beautiful. The answer was both the North and South islands. The concept: New Zealand. The world's two most beautiful islands.

They did this for a while but quickly tinkered their way into meaningless slogan land as the politics changed. Lucky for them, the country's beauty overcomes even the silliest slogan.

Products That Do Too Much

For many years, I've been writing about sacrifice. In other words, to get something, you have to give up something. Trying to be everything for everybody clearly undermines a clear perception of what makes you special or different. As mentioned earlier, if Volvo is to preempt *safety*, they can't be a convertible or a fancy looking car that tries to compete with BMW and Mercedes. And they have to innovate new safety ideas.

Convergence is the opposite of sacrifice; it is all about products that do more. And it's hard to avoid predictions about converging products in the worlds of computing, communications, consumer electronics, entertainment, and publishing.

These predictions go way back. A July 18, 1993, cover story in *Newsday* predicted that convergence would cause the eventual demise of videotapes, video stores, newspapers, TV channels, telephone operators, Yellow Pages, mail-order catalogs, college textbooks, library card catalogs, beepers, VCRs, checkbooks, and cassette players.

(We suspect you've noticed that many of these things that were predicted to go away are still alive and well. So much for that prediction.)

More recent predictions have telephones, video, and the Internet all converging at our television sets. Even the cartoonists are getting into the act. Our favorite has a gentleman, with his large-screen Sony on his shoulder saying hello into it.

If you study history, convergence rarely happens. Products that do more than they should are quick to die.

In 1937, we had the convertoplane, a combination helicopter and airplane that never got off the ground. Neither did the 1945 Hall Flying Car or the 1947 Taylor Aerocar.

In 1961, Amphicar was the first combination boat and automobile. The idea sank. (People figured they could just as easily park their boat at the marina and get into their car and drive home.)

In recent times, we had AT&T's EO personal communicator, a cellular phone, fax, electronic mail, personal organizer, and pen-based computer. Then there was Okidata's Doc-it, a desktop printer, fax, scanner, and copier. Finally we were introduced to a PDA, or Apple's Newton that was a message pad, a fax, beeper, calendar keeper, and pen-based computer. All of these are no longer with us. In this case, more is dead.

In a *New York Times* article, "The Case of the Subpar Smartphone," Joe Nocera brilliantly outlined the battles underway in the world of smartphones. Palm was wildly successful in the world of organizers. Then they introduced the unreliable and unremarkable Treo, an organizer that makes phone calls as well. As Ryan Block, the editor of the consumer electronics web site Engadget.com observed, "Palm has lost its way." They are not alone.

BlackBerrys are great at e-mail but the phone is barely adequate. The Motorola Q crashes almost as often as the Treo. The Apple iPhone is terrific for music and media but lousy for e-mail and phoning. For marketing reasons, everybody is trying to cram all these complicated features into ever-sleeker, ever-thinner boxes, while also adding longer battery life, and so on. Invariably, smartphone designers have to make compromises that mean some functions don't work especially well.

There is also the issue of heritage. All the big smartphone companies are coming at the device from a different starting point. Motorola has its roots in cell phones; not surprisingly, that's what works best on the Motorola Q. Apple has the iPod and computing in its heritage, so it does music and media really well. BlackBerry began as a mobile e-mail company, which is why its e-mail is so much better than everybody else's.

Creating products that do more than one thing requires sacrifice of a different kind. Designing multifunctional products forces your designers to give up what could be an outstanding single-function design for a lesser design that accommodates the extra functions.

Can a great car be a great boat at the same time? Of course not. If you want a really fast car, get a Ferrari. A fast boat? Get a Cigarette boat.

Can a great Formula One racing tire be a great passenger car tire at the same time? Of course not. (Racing tires don't have any tread.)

People want the best of the breed, not a mutt that contains several breeds.

People don't want to give up important features so that they can do other things with it. Just because you can build it offers no assurance that people will buy it.

If your difference is that your product can do a lot of things not very well as opposed to a product that does one thing exceptionally well, you haven't got much of a difference.

Brand Schizophrenia

Powerful brands have distinct personalities: Duracell's batteries last a long time. Dove contains cleansing cream. But even dominant brands can fade if they fall prey to multiple personality disorder. Consider General Motors. What's the difference between a Chevrolet, a Pontiac, and a Buick? The company appears to have woken up to the problem as they announced it would narrow its selection of cars. But this belated effort to bring the automaker's brand schizophrenia under control is too little too late.

General Motors mucked up their brands over decades of endless line extensions. But Mercedes-Benz has done it in less than one decade. Once upon a time, they had a high-quality, highly engineered, prestigious car. But now, if you wander into a dealership in Europe, you're faced with the following lineup: A-Class, B-Class, C-Class, E-Class, S-Class, CLK, CLS, CL, SLK, SL, M-Class, and G-Class. The prices ranges from 20,000 to 200,000 Euros. The result is that in Europe, Mercedes-Benz is not listed as the top brand. Audi A8, BMW, Maserati, and Jaguar have taken over this position.

The GM and Mercedes stories are not unique. Once a company abandons its brands' distinctive personalities or positions, it's just a matter of time before confused customers start to drift away. In 1985, Coca-Cola infamously introduced an identity-blurring new brand, New Coke. A massive consumer backlash ensued, and the company quickly reinstated its familiar Classic Coke. You'd think Coca-Cola would have learned from that experience the importance of having a unique product personality. But today the company sells 16 versions of Coke including such strange variations as Coca-Cola Zero, Diet Coke Plus, and Coca-Cola C2. What's a Coke? It's no wonder the company has lost its fizz.

There are ways to execute line extensions without confusing, and losing, your customers. What these strategies share is rigorous attention to the brand's *position*—consumers' sense of the brand's distinct, overarching identity. BMW, for example, has been "the ultimate driving machine," for decades, an identity that transcends the company's multiple product lines. Managed carefully, a good position is timeless. The "ultimate driving machine" is now 36 years old, "Marlboro Country" is 54, and "a diamond is forever" is 60.

What you have to fight off is the tendency for marketing people to tinker with a brand. After all, how else can they make their mark? As I said earlier, a marketing person rarely arrives at a new assignment and says, "Things look pretty good, let's not touch a thing." The next thing you know, you're about to come down with a bad case of brand schizophrenia.

But what's worse is a marketing executive who announces that brand schizophrenia is a good thing. Such was the case with

Larry Light, the ex-chief marketing officer of McDonald's, when in a speech he said that "Brand Chronicles" or multiple messages (i.e., personalities) was the way to go as opposed to brand positioning.

Should BMW abandon their long-term positioning strategy of being "The ultimate driving machine"? Should they go the way of Chevrolet, whose drive to be everything for everybody has resulted in their becoming nothing in the mind? (What's a Chevrolet?)

Positioning is how you differentiate yourself. Staying focused on that position is how you survive in a brutally competitive world. Ever since Coca-Cola dropped its heritage positioning strategy of "The Real Thing," things haven't gone well for Coke. Luckily, Pepsi leaving their youth positioning strategy of "Choice of the New Generation" kept things from getting worse.

Has it ever occurred to you that McDonald's was looking for slogans and not a positioning strategy? There's one that's right on the bottom of their sign that announces how many hamburgers they've served. McDonald's, with its international reach and billions of hamburgers served is staring at what I would call a very powerful, leadership positioning strategy. And, it's the one that would indeed encompass what they describe as a multidimensional brand.

The obvious positioning strategy: **"The World's favorite place to eat."**

I'm sorry, Larry, "Brand Chronicles" are not the way of the future. It's only a way of turning a brand that stands for something into a brand that stands for nothing.

6

An Obvious Look at the Marketing Process

If marketing people are to do a better job, they have to have a clear understanding of the marketing process—what's important and how to evaluate and operate the functions in which they are in charge.

Marketing's Importance

Long ago, Peter Drucker, considered the father of business consulting, made a profound observation that has been lost in the sands of time. He said, "Because the purpose of business is to create a customer, the business enterprise has two—and only two—basic functions: marketing and innovation. Marketing and innovation produce results; all the rest are costs. Marketing is the distinguishing, unique function of the business."

Today, when top management is surveyed, the order of their priorities is: finance, sales, production, management, legal, and people. Missing from the list: marketing and innovation. When you consider the trouble that many of our icons have run into in recent years, it is easy to surmise that Drucker's advice might have helped top management avoid the problems they face today.

Ironically, David Packard of Hewlett-Packard fame once observed, "Marketing is too important to be left to the marketing people." But as the years rolled on, rather than learn about marketing and innovation, executives started to search for role models instead of marketing models.

Tom Peters probably gave this trend a giant boost with the very successful book he co-authored, *In Search of Excellence*. Excellence, as defined in that book, didn't equal longevity, however; many of the role models offered there have since foundered. In retrospect, a better title for the book might have been *In Search of Strategy*.

A very popular method-by-example book has been *Built to Last* by James Collins and Jerry Porras. In it, they write glowingly about "Big Hairy Audacious Goals" that turned the likes of Boeing, Wal-Mart, General Electric, IBM, and others into the successful giants they have become.

The companies that these authors suggest for emulation were founded from 1812 (Citicorp) to 1945 (Wal-Mart). These firms didn't have to deal with the intense competition in today's global economy. While there is much you can learn from their success, they had the luxury of growing up when business life was a lot simpler. As a result, these role models are not very useful for companies today.

Today, there is a growing legion of competitors coming at them from every corner of the globe. Technologies are ever changing. The pace of change is faster than ever. It is increasingly difficult for CEOs to digest the flood of information out there and make the right choices.

But a CEO can have a future.

The trick to surviving out there is not to stare at the balance sheet but simply to know where you must go to find success in a market. No one can follow you (the board, your managers, your employees) if *you* don't know where you're headed.

How do you find the proper direction? To become a great strategist, you have to put your mind in the battlefront of the marketplace. You have to find your inspiration down at the front, in the ebb and flow of the great marketing battles taking place in the mind of the prospects. The following is a four-step process to pursue.

Step 1: Make Sense in the Context

Arguments are never made in a vacuum. You are always surrounded by competitors trying to make arguments of their own. Your message has to make sense in the context of the category. It has to start with what the marketplace has heard and registered from your competition.

What you really want to get is a quick snapshot of the perceptions that exist in the mind of your customers.

What you're after are the perceptual strengths and weaknesses of you and your competitors as they exist in the minds of the target group of customers.

Step 2: Find the Differentiating Idea

To be different is not to be the same. To be unique is to be one of a kind.

You're looking for something that separates you from your competitors. The secret to this is understanding that your differentness does not have to be product related.

Consider a horse. Horses are quickly differentiated by their type—racehorses, hunters, Tennessee walkers, American saddle, and on and on. You can differentiate any one group by breeding, performance, stable, trainer, and on and on. The same thing is true of your business as there are a number of different ways to differentiate a business beyond just focusing on your product.

Step 3: Have the Credentials

There are many ways to set your company or product apart. Let's just say the trick is to find that difference and then use it to set up a benefit for your customer.

To build a logical argument for your difference, you must have the credentials to support your differentiating idea, to make it real and believable.

If you have a product difference, then you should be able to demonstrate that difference. The demonstration, in turn, becomes your credentials. If you have a leak-proof valve, then you should be able to make a direct comparison with valves that can leak.

Claims of difference without proof are really just claims. For example, a wide-track Pontiac must be wider than other cars. British Air as the "world's favorite airline" should transport more people than any other airline. Mercedes should have superb engineering.

You can't differentiate with smoke and mirrors. Consumers are skeptical. They're thinking, "Oh yeah, Mr. Advertiser? Prove it!" You must be able to support your argument.

It's not exactly like being in a court of law. It's more like being in the court of public opinion.

Step 4: Communicate Your Difference

Just as you can't keep your light under a basket, you can't keep your difference under wraps.

If you build a differentiated product, the world will not automatically beat a path to your door. Better products don't win. Better perceptions tend to be the winners. News of your product has to have some help along the way.

Every aspect of your communications should reflect your difference—your advertising, your brochures, your web site, your sales presentations.

There's a lot of hogwash in corporate America about employee motivation brought to you by the "peak performance" crowd, along with their expensive pep rallies.

The folks who report to you don't need mystical answers to the question: "How do I unlock my true potential?" The question they need answered is: "What makes this company different?"

That answer gives them something to latch on to and run with, *especially if it's obvious*.

Marketing Simplified

I'm beginning to think that many of the marketing mistakes you read about are caused by the simple fact that many marketing people are hopelessly confused. And, as time goes by, more information adds to the confusion.

Academics have written tomes about the complexity of marketing and all its functions. Ad agencies and consultants have constructed convoluted systems for building brands. One of my favorite pieces of complexity comes from a U.K. consulting firm that claims a brand has nine positioning elements in a customer's mind: functional needs, objective effects, functional roles, attributes, core evaluators, psychological drives, psychological roles, subjective character, and psychological needs. Then the consultants turn all this into a "bridge matrix." (Help, I'm trapped on a bridge to nowhere.)

One marketing firm came out with a book that talks about the "ecosystem of consumer demand." They offer a four-step process:

1. Map the demand landscape,
2. Explore consumption motivations,
3. Reframe the opportunity space, and
4. Quantify the sweet spot.

The objective of all this jargon is to fit your product into the changing ecosystem of everyday life, transforming how people live, work, and play. (Help, I have no idea what they are talking about.)

I'll give you the essence of marketing in two sentences:

First, it's marketing's responsibility to see that everyone is playing the same tune in unison.

Second, it's marketing's assignment to turn that tune or differentiating idea into what we call a *coherent marketing direction.*

The notion of a differentiating idea requires some thought. What kind of idea? Where do you find one? These are the initial questions that must be answered.

To help you answer these questions, I propose using the following specific definition: *A differentiating idea is a competitive mental angle.*

This kind of idea must have a *competitive* angle in order to have a chance for success. This does not necessarily mean a better product or service, but rather there must be an element of differentness. It could be smaller, bigger, lighter, heavier, cheaper, or more expensive. It could be a different distribution system.

Furthermore, the idea must be competitive in the total marketing arena, not just competitive in relation to one or two other products or services. For example, Volkswagen's decision in the late 1950s to introduce the first "small" car was an excellent competitive idea. At the time, General Motors was manufacturing nothing but big, heavily chromed patrol boats. The Beetle was a runaway success. It was an obvious idea.

The VW Beetle was not the first small car on the market, of course. But it was the first car to occupy the "small" position in the minds of consumers. It made a virtue out of its size, while others apologized for their small size by talking about "roominess."

"Think small," said the Volkswagen ads. (Now there's an obvious idea.)

Second, a differentiating idea must have a competitive *mental* angle. In other words, the battle takes place in the mind of the prospect.

Competitors that do not exist in the mind can be ignored. There were plenty of pizza places with home delivery operations when John Schnatter launched Papa John's. But nobody owned the "better ingredients" position in the mind.

A competitive mental *angle* is the point in the mind that allows your marketing program to work effectively. That's the point you must leverage to achieve results. But an idea is not enough. To complete the process, you need to turn the idea into a strategy.

What's a strategy? A strategy is not a goal. Like life itself, a strategy ought to focus on the journey, not the goal. Top-down thinkers are goal-oriented. They first determine what it is they want to achieve, and then they try to devise ways and means to achieve their goals.

But most goals are simply not achievable. Goal setting tends to be an exercise in frustration. Marketing, like politics, is the art of the possible.

Roger Smith took over General Motors (GM) in 1981; he predicted that GM would eventually own 70 percent of the traditional Big Three domestic car market, up from about 66 percent in 1979. To prepare for this awesome responsibility, GM began a $50 billion modernization program. Boy, was Roger wrong. Currently, GM's share of the Big Three domestic market is 28 percent and falling. His goal was simply not achievable because it was not based on a sound idea.

In my definition, a strategy is not a goal. It's a *coherent marketing direction*. A strategy is *coherent* in the sense that it is focused on the idea that has been selected. Volkswagen had a big tactical success with the small car, but it failed to elevate this idea to a coherent strategy. It forgot about "small" and instead elected to bring into the U.S. market a family of big, fast, and expensive Volkswagens. But other car manufacturers had already preempted these automotive ideas. This opened the way for the Japanese to take over the small car idea.

Second, a strategy encompasses coherent *marketing* activities. Product, pricing distribution, advertising—all of the activities that make up the marketing mix must be coherently focused on the idea. (Think of a differentiating idea as a particular wavelength of light and the strategy as a laser tuned to that wavelength. You need both to penetrate the mind of the prospect.)

Finally, a strategy is a coherent marketing *direction*. Once the strategy is established, the direction shouldn't be changed.

The purpose of the strategy is to mobilize your resources to preempt the differentiating idea. By committing all your resources to one strategic direction, you maximize the exploitation of the idea without the limitation that the existence of a goal implies.

How to Evaluate Advertising

In a meeting of the Association of Advertising, the basic theme proclaimed was that advertising won't work unless it's creative.

That is the same old saw that the agencies have been pushing for decades. It all starts with a client meeting with lots of charts, pretty pictures, smoke, not much strategy, and a hefty budget.

What's a client to do? If you've ever been put into this position, here's a short course on how to evaluate advertising.

First of all, advertising is what you do when you can't go to see somebody personally. You send a television commercial or a print ad to tell your story. Any ad program has to start with the product difference you are trying to communicate. Why buy my product instead of someone else's? You're not after a meaningless slogan. Your program has to contain that difference and the benefit that comes with it.

Most agencies today will pitch that advertising has to form a bond with the customer. The customers have to like the advertising, which means you can't sell too hard. Liking advertising is only useful if you're selling tickets to watch it.

Don't buy into all that. As I wrote earlier, the basic role of an agency is to take that difference and make it interesting by dramatizing it. People are attracted to the media because of its entertainment and information value, not because they are dying to see your latest ad. The agency can use sex or humor or whatever, but the ad must communicate that reason to buy. If you like the way the agency did that, approve it. Or ask for more drama.

A good example was Pepsi-Cola's introductory advertising for their Aquafina brand of water. The differentiating idea is guaranteed purity, which is right on the label. The commercial shows nothing but pure water and the brand. The verbal message describes the product as "pure nothing." They did a brilliant job of dramatizing nothing.

It's important to realize that people know an ad when they see one. And since these ads are usually interrupting what people are watching or reading, they are not too happy about being forced to watch them. No one likes to be sold. So a little candor goes a long way. This kind of honesty is very disarming. People will often give you a positive response if you're candid with them. If your widget is a little ugly, admit it. But then go on to say it's very reliable. People will buy it. That's exactly what Bill Bernbach communicated years ago when he started writing the advertising for the VW Beetle. They admitted the car was small and ugly, but they also told people it was reliable. This wasn't creativity. It was candor and brilliant strategy.

To me one of the most candid and effective current programs is the one that Boar's Head is running to advertise its 350 deli products. They candidly compare their high-quality meats to their competitors' products. Their concept is simple, "Almost Boar's Head isn't Boar's Head." They've convinced people to spend a lot more per pound to get that quality.

Another tip is to try to make your message sound like big news. People are always looking for news. News is very disarming, and people let down their "being sold" defenses. Believe me, if you start an advertisement with an announcer saying, "Before you push that button on your remote, I have some important news for you," you would freeze every viewer in his or her chair.

Also, beware of complexity; you're not going to get much time from people so you must keep your advertising simple. One message is better than two messages. Simple visuals are better than dramatic visuals. And here's a simple trick: Rhyme things if you can. It makes your words much more memorable. Why do you think people remember poetry more than prose? It's the rhyme. Ralph Waldo Emerson put it perfectly when he said, "The road to the heart is the ear."

Most important, you're in search of that obvious idea I've been preaching. This is apt to be so simple and commonplace that it has no appeal to the imagination. As I've written, humans all like clever ideas but the obvious idea is the one most likely to work well.

To sum up, when you're evaluating advertising, avoid meaningless slogans and look for your product's difference. Then judge how well the ad dramatizes that difference, how honest the message is, how simply the message is presented, and whether there is some interesting news for your customer that translates into a benefit. If the advertising does some or all of that, it's good. If not, it's bad. Then, be patient and let the ad work.

Advertising takes time to register with people. So you have to stay with your message for a long enough time for them to get it. When you're bored with the message, your customers will probably just begin to notice and remember it.

If you're interested in more on this subject, you might try and find an excellent little book titled, *The Ad Contrarian*. It was written by Bob Hoffman.

How to Evaluate Logos

The prior section was about evaluating advertising, a business expense that can be very expensive and wasteful if not done right. I thought it might be useful to offer some thoughts on evaluating another potentially wasteful and expensive process: corporate identity or logos.

If you've ever been in a corporate identity or logo meeting, you'll hear terms like glyphs, monoseals, or dramatic angles. Colors are given feelings, shapes become dynamic or elegant or sensual. It can all be very confusing. So let's start at the beginning in an effort to clear things up.

Logos have been with us for thousands of years. A Babylonian clay tablet from about 3000 BC bears inscriptions for an ointment dealer and a shoemaker. The Roman legions had them. In the Middle Ages, every two-bit Duke with a handful of knights had one plastered on his shield. There were crests or coats of arms everywhere. But none ever amounted to anything. What lived on were the names of the people involved or the places the big battles were fought. What does that tell you?

It's not about the symbol. It's about the name connected to the symbol.

You might say, "What about the famous Nike swoosh I see on all those athletic shoes, shorts, and shirts?"

It's the Nike name that gives meaning to the swoosh symbol. But they've spent hundreds of millions of dollars to link the two so they can put it on clothing and not be quite as pushy with their name. It's really only a stand-in for the name.

Ironically, it's the success of Nike that leads companies to say, "I want one of those." Unfortunately, I once saw a piece of research on names and logos versus just the logos with the names taken away. You would be amazed at just how few logos are recognized without the name—only a handful. Yet, millions of dollars have been spent on logos like the General Electric monogram, the CBS eye, or the Mercedes three-pointed star. And these symbols took years to establish. Your brand-new symbol probably has no chance of standing alone without your name.

Take the most successful logos such as Mobil or Hertz or IBM. All of those feature the name, not the symbol. Mobil has a red O. Hertz and Federal Express have unique typography. The symbol that comes with American Airlines is simply AA with a set of wings in the middle. You could say that, in designing a logo, the name is the game.

There are other considerations in designing a logo. One is the shape. It should be rectangular because that is how you can see it best. If it's too vertical or too horizontal, it's not as readable. The biggest mistake people make is allowing their logos to be hard to read.

Some people, if you can believe it, use symbols that are bigger than the name. Others let designers pick a typeface to express what they feel are the attributes of the brand rather than the typeface's ability to be read quickly. Some choose typefaces that are illegible. Legibility is the most important aspect to look for in selecting a logo.

Take Absolut Vodka. Their unique bottle shape is really their logo. And they've dramatized it with their visual advertising on the shape.

The Jaguar automobile also has a unique shape that functions like a logo that people quickly recognize. Jaguar is now owned by Ford and I'm beginning to see that shape being modified. That could be an enormous mistake.

Color can also be important in a corporation's identity. For example: Warm colors, such as red, orange, and yellow, tend to jump out at you and attract attention. They have high energy and are good for retail. Blues are cool and conservative. They recede from view and are considered upscale. Bright colors are often described as casual and playful.

You preempt a color so that it becomes part of your identity.

Hertz is yellow. Avis is red. Kodak is yellow. Fuji is green. Coke is red. Pepsi is blue. FedEx is red and purple. UPS is brown. Color can be a useful way to identify your brand. Just make sure you don't pick your competitor's color.

You might ask, what about logos that aren't full names? Like initials? Here is where you have to be careful. Initials only make good logos if they are nicknames of an established company name. General Electric is a long name so GE makes an excellent logo, because it's what people will use as a nickname. The same goes for FedEx instead of Federal Express or IBM instead of International Business Machines. Can you imagine trying to drag around a name like Minnesota Mining and Manufacturing? It's no wonder they became the 3M Company.

But remember, nicknames are given to you by the marketplace. It should be what people tend to call you. Don't try to force it. If people tend to use your full name, that's your name and that's what should be your logo. Metropolitan Life Insurance can be MetLife. But New York Life will always be New York Life.

So there you have it. In picking a logo, it's all about the name, and making sure it's readable. The color and the typography are far more important than some meaningless symbol unless that symbol represents your nickname—and remember, your nickname is only a nickname if it is used.

Minds Hate to Change

Three news items caught my attention.

One was about how Viacom discovered that kids don't want their MTV online. It seems that the kids didn't follow from cable to their online offering called "MTV Overdrive." (The numbers tell this tale. They generated less than 4 million viewers as compared to MySpace, which gets 55 million unique visitors, and fast-growing YouTube, which garners 16 million viewers. Viacom's television show gets 82 million monthly viewers.)

The next article was about how paper coupons are holding their own against the online competition. One would think that with the Internet's ability to aim at narrow groups of consumers, it would easily begin to make progress against those Sunday newspapers loaded with coupons that you have to cut out. It turns out that slow and old is holding its own against fast and new.

Finally, there are the current problems of that powerhouse brand Dell. Among their problems, I noticed their inability to move into consumer electronics with TVs and music players. It turns out that their solid brand image doesn't help in the fast-growing consumer markets.

What's going on here? Well, dear readers, these three companies have run up against a basic fact of life: Minds don't change. MTV is something you watch on television. Coupons are something you cut out. And Dell is a business computer you buy direct. The futility of trying to change minds in the marketplace is a lesson I learned many years ago.

Those were the days when I was trying to drag the perceptions of Western Union into the twentieth century. We tried advertising everything from satellite launches to advanced communications services. Nothing worked.

After years of effort, the consumer's perception of Western Union as the old-fashioned telegraph company was as strong as ever. The final advice: Change the company name to Westar, and use the Western Union brand only on the telegraph and money-order services. Anything else was hopeless. While the advice was good, our message wasn't well received.

Since that time, I've watched many others blow a lot of money on trying to change minds in the marketplace. Xerox lost hundreds of millions trying to convince the market that Xerox machines that didn't make copies were worth the money. No one would buy their computers.

Volkswagen dropped over 60 share points trying to convince the market that VW wasn't just a small, reliable, economical car like the Beetle. No one bought their big or expensive fast cars.

Prell, the famous green shampoo, decided to introduce a blue version. People preferred green, not blue.

Pepsi-Cola thought they had a brilliant idea in the form of a clear cola. No one who bought Pepsi-Cola thought that was a good idea.

When the market makes up its mind about a product, there's no changing that mind. As the late John Kenneth Galbraith once said, "Faced with the choice between changing one's mind and proving that there is no need to do so, almost everyone gets busy on the proof."

Another finding supports how minds are more comfortable with what they know. A general feeling in the marketing industry has always been that new-product advertising should generate higher interest than advertising for established brands. But it turns out that we're actually more impressed by what we already know (or buy) than by what's "new."

One research organization, McCollum Speilman, has tested more than 22,000 TV commercials over 23 years. Almost 6,000 of those commercials were for new products in 10 product categories.

What did they learn? Greater persuasion ability and attitude shifts—the so-called "new-product excitement"—were evident in only *one* of the 10 categories (pet products) when comparing new brands to established brands.

In the other nine categories—ranging from drugs to beverages to personal hygiene items—there was no real difference, no burst of excitement, enabling consumers to distinguish between established brands and new brands.

With thousands of different commercials across hundreds of different brands, you can pretty much rule out creativity as the difference in persuasion. It comes back to what we're familiar with—what we're already comfortable with.

In the book *The Reengineering Revolution*, MIT professor-turned-consultant Michael Hammer calls human beings' innate resistance to change "the most perplexing, annoying, distressing, and confusing part" of reengineering.

To help us better understand this resistance, a book titled *Attitudes and Persuasion* offers some insights. Authors Richard Petty and John Cacioppo spend some time on "belief systems." Here's their take on why minds are so hard to change:

> The nature and structure of belief systems is important from the perspective of an informational theorist, because beliefs are thought to provide the cognitive foundation of an attitude. (p. 184)

To change an attitude, it is presumably necessary to modify the information on which that attitude rests. It is generally necessary, therefore, to change a person's beliefs, eliminate old beliefs, or introduce new beliefs.

That's right, you have to change beliefs. And you're going to do all that with a 30-second commercial?

So my advice to you marketing experts out there is that if your assignment is to change people's minds, don't accept the assignment.

Branding Simplified

Branding has become a subject in marketing that has been turned from a molehill into a mountain. It's a subject that has spread into areas far afield from the branding of products. Rock groups, movie stars, and even symphonies are talked about as brands. Maybe it's time to cut through all the silliness and clarify things.

The last time I looked, there were over 2,000 books covering some topic related to brands or branding. What used to be just the logo and the name of a product or company has now become this almost mystic creation that encompasses unique identities and qualities separate from the product names. There is an army of consultants trying to sell you some branding system or another. Forget all that. But let's begin at the beginning. As Walter Landor once said, "Products are created in the factory, but brands are created in the mind."

In the old days, a brand name was nothing more than a word in the mind. A proper noun that is spelled with a capital letter.

But today, there are almost two million brand names or trademarks registered with the U.S. government. To be successful, it helps a great deal to have a good name.

Despite this, companies continue to give themselves terrible names. The biggest mistake people make is to use initials such as USG, NCA, or AMP. These are Fortune 500 companies, but all-initial names are not really names at all. They're a one-way ticket to oblivion. Another problem occurs when companies take a good name and change it to a bad name.

The U.K. postal service renamed itself Consignia, a name that had no relevance to postal services. Fifteen months later, after endless jokes and ridicule in the media, it was changed back to their previous excellent name, the Royal Mail Group. A lot of time, effort, and money went into that mistake—not smart.

The best names are linked directly to a product benefit such as DieHard, a long-lasting battery, or Windex for window cleaning, or Intensive Care skin lotion.

Another tip is a name that sounds good such as Caress bath soap or NutraSweet sweetener. In many ways, the mind works by ear so you want to avoid strange-sounding, coined names like UNUM, Agilent, or Zylog. What you're after are nice sounding names like Humana or Acura.

Now, let's move to branding.

A branding program is all about differentiating your product or company from the others in your category. And, if you don't have a point of difference, you'd better have a very low price. An example is Toyota who, over many years, has established the powerful position as a "reliable" automobile. They have driven that differentiation idea to become the world's leading brand of automobiles.

You might ask, "Isn't that standard operating procedure for most marketers?"

Were it only so. A research firm called Copernicus investigated 48 pairs of leading brands in 48 different product and service categories. The objective was to measure whether brands were becoming more similar and commodity-like over time. Tragically, out of the 48 categories evaluated, 40 were perceived as becoming similar.

Three reasons were presented as to why this was happening. There's a shift from brand building to promotional programs or deals. There's a shift from informational-oriented advertising to entertainment-oriented advertising. (I've written a lot about this in earlier chapters.) In addition, there's a failure to communicate a distinctive point of difference. That moves the equation from branding to pricing. And let me tell you, the first people to exploit perceived similarity are the big mass merchandisers like Wal-Mart and Home Depot. They will put enormous pressure on you to reduce your prices. And they will get away with it if the shopper doesn't perceive a reason to pay a little more for your brand.

This raises another question: "Why do companies have trouble with this?"

The trick is to figure out how to express that difference. It's easy if you're faster or fancier or safer or new. But often you have to find other nonproduct attributes like leadership or preference or heritage. Whatever you select, use it to set up a benefit for your prospect. Many companies just don't understand this. All they promote are meaningless slogans. Michael Porter said it very well:

Competitive strategy is about being different. It means deliberately choosing a different set of activities to deliver a unique mix of value. The essence of strategy is in the activities—choosing to perform activities differently or to perform different activities than rivals. Otherwise, a strategy is nothing more than a marketing slogan that will not withstand competition. (p. 45)

So, if you want a simple definition of branding, here it is: *It's all about establishing a brand and a differentiating idea in the mind of your prospect.*

That said, it's not exactly that simple. There is a hard part about branding. It's called staying focused. The next section focuses on that subject.

Branding Simplified: The Bad News

In the prior section, I attempted to clarify what branding was all about. It came down to building perceptions about what makes you different and what the benefit is in this difference. Now for the bad news.

Building a brand is often easier than keeping it from being destroyed by internal forces.

This often happens because of the pressures that financial guys put on an organization. To make the numbers they want them to make, people start to do things that begin to unravel a brand.

To ratchet up more business, the organization starts to lose focus on what makes it unique. They do things that erode the core brand. They take the obvious and make it less obvious. They chase business they shouldn't chase, such as Marlboro trying to sell menthol cigarettes, or Cadillac trying to sell small Cadillacs. Sometimes, they create a subbrand, thinking it gives their new effort some legitimacy. Like Holiday Inn Crowne Plaza—the customers thought that the Crowne Plaza version was a little too expensive for a Holiday Inn. It never flew.

It's easy to see the problems of trying to go up-market with a down-market brand, but what about the reverse? That can be good news and bad news.

Waterford Crystal is trying that with Marquis by Waterford. The more successful the cheaper crystal becomes, the more it will erode the expensive Waterford brand. The same goes for Mercedes. The more cheap models they push, the more they will erode the prestige of the bigger, more expensive Mercedes. A brand is a promise. It creates the expectations that the product has to deliver.

You might ask, "Can a brand be marketed in more than one form or model?"

Sure, as long as the different forms or models don't detract from the essence of the brand or the concept that makes it different from other brands. If Heinz is a leading ketchup brand, a Heinz mustard makes no sense in the mind of a customer. If Nike is what the world's best athletes wear, a Nike golf ball doesn't make much sense. You certainly can't wear it. What's saved them is, that to many, it's the ball that Tiger Woods uses. A Tiger Woods golf ball has sold a whole lot better than a Nike golf ball.

Many ask me why these kinds of decisions get made?

The answer is greed. Quite often, new management arrives and, encouraged by Wall Street, they push the brand beyond where it should be pushed. Consider the latest marketing pronouncement from Volvo. They are asking agencies to take their advertising beyond safety. They claim, "Safety is not enough." Wrong. Safety is what they are and they're letting Japanese carmakers take the lead in electronic safety innovation. Volvo has got to get better at safety, not shift to emotion or some other vague nondifferentiating idea.

This leads me to the final question, "So how do you avoid losing focus and undermining your brand?"

The answer is *sacrifice*. Giving up something can be good for your business. When you study categories over a long period of time, you can see that adding more can weaken growth, not help it. The more you add, the more you risk undermining your basic differentiating idea. Sacrifice comes in three forms:

1. *Product sacrifice* or staying focused on one kind of product—Duracell in alkaline batteries, KFC in chicken, Southwest Airlines in short-haul air travel.

2. *Attribute sacrifice* or staying focused on one kind of product attribute—Nordstom on service, Dell on selling direct, Papa John's Pizza on better ingredients. Your product might offer more than one attribute, but your message should be focused on the one you want to preempt.

3. *Target market sacrifice* or staying focused on one target segment in a category enables you to become the preferred product in that segment—DeWalt for professional tools, Pepsi for the younger generation, Corvette for the generation that wants to be young. If you chase another segment, chances are you'll chase away your original customers.

So there it is in simple terms: Branding is putting a brand in the consumer's mind along with its point of difference. The trick is to stay focused on what the brand stands for and not get greedy with it.

When No One Is in Charge

This is an interesting time in the marketing world. First, *Time* magazine announces that the person of the year is "Us" or all of those folks blogging and chatting on the Internet undermining journalists, politicians, celebrities, and anyone that becomes a target.

Then, *Advertising Age* announces that the Agency of the Year is not an agency at all but the award goes to "Us" or all those folks videoing, blogging, and web siting on the Internet undermining the professionals in the agency business. They explained it by saying that the consumer is king and even though *Time* beat them to it, they were sticking with "Us." Here's *Advertising Age*'s explanation: "*Time* was picking consumer-generated content over world leaders, dictators with nuclear weapons, and people who are trying to save our broken planet. *Advertising Age* is picking 'Us' over the professional content creators."

Then I saw something that convinced me that indeed the inmates had taken over the asylum. It seems that amateurs are writing Super Bowl ads. That's right, some marketers are running Internet contests enabling consumer-generated advertising to appear in what is costing almost $3 million a spot in the Super Bowl.

What is going on here? Maybe it's time to review what the role of advertising is all about as well as the role of the advertising agency.

Marketing should be about how you differentiate your product in the mind of your customers and prospects. I've expressed this for many years in book after book, including this one. That's because marketing is not a battle of products, it's a battle of perceptions.

So the role of advertising is to drive that differentiating idea or perception into the mind. Here's an analogy that might be useful: Consider the differentiating idea as a nail that you want to drive into the mind. An advertising program in all its forms is the hammer you use to drive that idea into the mind.

That said, what does "Us" know about all that. We'll just come up with some form of clever commercial that probably will not include a reason to buy the product instead of the competitor's product. It will be the kind of commercial that will elicit the response of "what are they selling?" If a marketer clearly spells all that out in advance by saying to those consumers or amateurs that are generating this advertising, "Here's my point of difference, I want you to dramatize it," maybe you'll get something of value. But I tend to doubt it.

Effective advertising is a science that requires a great deal of experience and training. Sure there is a degree of art involved, but you should never let the art get in the way of a selling message. Most bad advertising is about entertainment, not selling. And I'm afraid that's the kind of stuff the inmates will want to produce. To them, *selling* is a dirty word.

Finally, a few thoughts about the Internet, where this so-called consumer revolution is taking place. As I've written earlier, we must be careful about all this so-called change. For example, I recently heard that some online companies are starting to use old-fashioned catalogs in their marketing efforts. That's unexpected to say the least.

Once again, what's going on here? Well, what companies are discovering is that the Internet is another tool, not the be-all and end-all of traditional media marketing. The catalogs are liberally loaded with web site mentions so that people can get more information. This takes some of the information load off the catalog. Thus, it can be designed better and be more of a story-telling or brand-building vehicle. They realize that the catalog does a better job at dramatizing their story and what they offer. And I suspect that none of "Us" are writing their catalogs for them.

To me, that sounds like a better way to run the asylum.

Some Help in That Search for the Obvious

The search should generally start with the competition. It's not what you want to do. It's what your competition will let you do. Also, you have to avoid making the kinds of mistakes often made. I'll also share two of my favorite obvious strategies.

Repositioning the Competition

This is one of my favorites and it is also a very powerful marketing strategy that has fallen into disuse. Why? I have no idea unless it's about creative people thinking that it's not creative. It's called "repositioning the competition," and my ex-partner Al Ries and I wrote about it in a book called *Positioning: The Battle for Your Mind*.

In simple terms, to move a new idea or product into the mind, you must first move an old one out. "The world is round," said Christopher Columbus. "No, it's not," said the public, "it's flat."

To convince the public otherwise, fifteenth-century scientists first had to prove that the world wasn't flat. One of their more convincing arguments was the fact that sailors at sea were first able to observe the tops of the masts of an approaching ship, then the sails, then the hull. If the world were flat, they would see the whole ship at once.

All the mathematical arguments in the world weren't as effective as a simple observation the public should verify themselves. Once an old idea is overturned, selling the new idea is often ludicrously simple. As a matter of fact, people will often actively search for a new idea to fill the void.

Never be afraid of conflict either. The crux of a repositioning program is undercutting an existing concept, product, or person. Conflict, even personal conflict, can build a reputation overnight. Where would Sam Ervin have been without Richard Nixon? (you younger folks missed this one.)

For that matter, where would Richard Nixon have been without Alger Hiss? And Ralph Nader got famous not by saying anything about Ralph Nader but by going out and attacking the world's largest corporation single-handedly.

People like to watch the bubble burst.

Tylenol went out and burst the aspirin bubble.

"For the millions who should not take aspirin," said Tylenol's ads. "If your stomach is easily upset . . . or you have an ulcer . . . or you suffer from asthma, allergies, or iron-deficiency anemia, it would make good sense to check with your doctor before you take aspirin."

"Aspirin can irritate the stomach lining," continued the Tylenol ad, "trigger asthmatic or allergic reactions, cause small amounts of hidden gastrointestinal bleeding."

"Fortunately, there is Tylenol . . ."

Sixty words of copy before any mention of the advertiser's product. Sales of Tylenol acetaminophen took off. Today

Tylenol is the No.1 brand of analgesic. A simple but effective repositioning strategy did the job against an institution like aspirin. Amazing.

Stolichnaya burst the American vodka bubble.

"Most American vodkas seem Russian," said the ads. And the captions said: "Samovar: Made in Schenley, Pennsylvania. Smirnoff: Made in Hartford, Connecticut. Wolfschmidt: Made in Lawrenceburg, Indiana. Stolichnaya is different. It is Russian and it is made in Leningrad." (Now St. Petersburg.)

One of Procter & Gamble's most powerful programs was the one that launched Scope mouthwash. Procter & Gamble used two words to reposition Listerine, the king of Halitosis Hill: "Medicine breath." Who wants their breath to smell like a hospital?

Over 20 years ago, BMW launched its very successful car by repositioning Mercedes. The headline of the introductory ad said, "The ultimate sitting machine verses the ultimate driving machine." Who wants just a living room on wheels?

The success of the Tylenol, Scope, Stolichnaya, and other repositioning programs has spawned a host of similar advertising. Too often, however, these copycat campaigns have missed the essence of repositioning strategy.

"We're better than our competitors" isn't repositioning. It's comparative advertising and not very effective. There's a psychological flaw in the advertiser's reasoning that the prospect is quick to detect. "If your brand is so good, how come it's not the leader?"

A look at comparative ads suggests why most of them aren't effective. They fail to reposition the competition.

Rather, they use the competitor as a benchmark for their own brand. Then they tell the reader or viewer how much better they are. Which, of course, is exactly what the prospect expects the advertiser to say.

Ban deodorant once ran an ad that said, "Ban is more effective than Right Guard, Secret, Sure, Arrid Extra Dry, Mitchum, Soft & Dry, Body All, and Dial." The reader looks at an ad like this and asks, "What else is new?"

Ironically, where this strategy is alive and well is in the land of politics. Karl Rove did enormous damage to John Kerry by repositioning him as a "flip-flopper." This helped George Bush set up his position of being a strong leader. Unfortunately, the Kerry campaign was too busy trying to position him as a Vietnam War hero instead of attacking the Bush record. They should have used repositioning against the Bush strategy by saying that President Bush was "strong but wrong."

Interestingly, I had an opportunity to turn the tables on Mr. Rove. In working with Nancy Pelosi during the 2006 elections, I recommended that the Democrats should use an obvious repositioning strategy against the Republicans. My suggestion: Hang "incompetent" on the Bush administration and Republican party. That's exactly what they did and you all know how it worked out.

Coping with the Competition

I've been in this marketing business for over 40 years. I've seen the good old times and the difficult new times. When people ask me what has changed, my response is one word: competition. What I thought was a competitive marketplace, today looks like a tea party. Everybody is after everybody's business.

Because of this ugly fact of life, the key to survival is to start every marketing plan with your competition in mind. It's not what you want to do, it's what your competition will let you do. In the next two sections, I'll give you survival tips in your search for an obvious strategy.

Avoid a Competitor's Strength and Exploit Their Weakness

When a competitor is known for one thing, you have to be known for something else. Quite often, a competitor's built-in weakness is the something else that you can exploit. If McDonald's strength is that of being a little kid's place, Burger King can exploit that by being a grown-up place. For years, Detroit's automobiles were perceived as not being very reliable. Toyota was able to exploit these perceptions and take ownership of the attribute of "reliability."

But remember, we're talking strength and weakness in the minds of the marketplace. Marketing is a battle of perceptions. What you're really doing is exploiting perceptions.

Always Be a Little Bit Paranoid about Competition

We're living in a world where everyone is after everyone's business. You have to realize that one of your competitors is probably in a meeting figuring out how to nail you in some way or another. You must constantly be gathering information on what your competitors are planning. This can come from an astute salesforce or a friendly customer or from some research.

Never underestimate your competitor. In fact, you're safer if you overestimate them. AT&T, DEC, Levi's, and Crest are testimony to underestimating the kind of damage competitors can do even to market leaders.

Competitors Will Usually Get Better, If Pushed

Companies who figure they can exploit a sloppy competitor make big mistakes. They ridicule their competitor's product or service and say they can do things better. Then, lo and

behold, their big competitor suddenly improves and that so-
called advantage melts away.

No. 2 Avis did indeed try harder, but Hertz quickly
improved their efforts. Then one day they ran a devastating
ad with the headline: *For years, Avis has been telling you they
are No. 2. Now we're going to tell you why.*

Then they went on to list all their improvements. Avis
never quite recovered. Never build your program around your
competitor's mistakes. They will correct them in short order.

When Business Is Threatened, Competitors Aren't Rational

Survival is a powerful instinct in life and in business. When
threatened, all rationality goes out the window. I have a favorite story about this tendency.

A start-up company came up with a unique packaging system for baby carrots that produced a decided price advantage
over the two big suppliers already in the business.

To get on the supermarket shelves, they entered the market
not with better carrots but with a better price, which the
established brands immediately matched. This only forced the
new company to go lower, which once again was matched by
their competitors.

When a board member asked the management of the start-
up to predict what would happen, the management predicted
that the two big companies would not continue to reduce
their prices because it was "irrational." They were losing
money because of their older packaging technology.

The board member called me about the prediction. I
advised him that they would continue to be irrational until
they forced this new upstart out of the market. Why would
they make it easy for a new company that threatened their
stable business?

At the next board meeting, the start-up company management was encouraged to sell their new manufacturing system to one of the established brands. They did this for a nice profit.

So much for companies being rational.

Know Your Enemy

The last section gave you four tips on developing your marketing plan, everything from exploiting a competitor's weakness to never underestimating the competition. Here are four more.

Coping with the competition isn't getting any easier. If you want to pursue the subject further, I suggest you pick up a copy of *Marketing Warfare*, a book my ex-partner and I wrote over 20 years ago. (In fact, there's a 20th anniversary edition.) It lays out a competitive model on just what your strategy should be based on your position in the marketplace. It's all about knowing your enemy.

Squash Your Smaller Competitors as Quickly as Possible

In war, the generals have an important maxim about being attacked:

> The best place to deal with an invading force is to get them in the water where they have the least maneuverability. Next, attack them on the beaches where they have limited maneuverability. But most of all, don't let them get inland where they can develop momentum.

So it is in business: You must move against your smaller competitors as soon as possible so they cannot develop legitimacy and momentum. General Motors hung back when the Germans and Japanese invaded the U.S. market with small cars. They felt they couldn't make money on this type of car so they quickly rationalized their position by convincing themselves that Americans wanted big comfortable cars. Wrong.

Gillette, on the other hand, countered BIC's disposable razors with the twin-bladed disposable called Good News. They may not make much money on these razors, but today they dominate this category as well as the traditional and more profitable category of cartridge razors.

But you have to be careful here. No one squashed competition better than Microsoft. My advice: Keep squashing until you hear from the feds. Then apologize and back off a bit.

If You've Got a Bigger Competitor, Avoid Being Squashed

Here's the other side of the coin. How do you avoid a big competitor that has just taken my advice?

In two words, be careful.

The best strategy is to sneak up on a bigger competitor early on and never appear to be threatening. Slowly build your business and momentum in places where you're less visible. After you've got some size and momentum, you can step up and better deal with the bigger players.

Wal-Mart got its start in lightly populated counties of the United States where the main competitors were mom-and-pop retailers. Only after it built size and momentum did it move into the heavily populated counties where it confronted the other big mass merchandisers.

Sono-Site pioneered small, hand-held ultrasound devices that could compete with big expensive ultrasound machines built by General Electric. They quietly developed a global presence before General Electric could get into the small machine game. Today, they are almost a generic brand.

Southwest Airlines pursued a similar strategy of slowly building their route structure in nonhub airports and limited routes. It started in Texas, moved to the West Coast, then spread into the Midwest, and now is working its way around the East. By the time the big airlines challenged it, Southwest had real momentum. And Herb Kelleher maintained some real differences from his bigger competitors that kept his costs down: no food, no reservations, no hubs, and just one kind of plane. Now he runs Super Bowl ads, is highly visible, and is kicking butt.

If You're Losing the Battle, Shift the Battlefield

A company that takes a licking will *not* keep ticking. (Only a Timex watch does that.) Even companies with deep pockets will suffer in this very competitive world. A better approach is to shift your efforts to a place where you can take better advantage of your strengths.

By manufacturing in the United States, Levi's couldn't compete on price with the me-too jeans manufacturers. By shifting to an authentic or original strategy, they could have played to their strength while making the case of paying a little more for the jeans. And it also would have given them time to shift manufacturing offshore.

Kellogg's Corn Flakes is winning the battle against Cheerios with its current strategy. Shifting the focus to "real cereal" puts the issue in a context that favors Kellogg's, a company that makes its cereal the old-fashioned way, not the processed way.

You want to move the marketplace to a point where you can use your point of difference against your competitor instead of being hammered by your competitor's point of difference.

If a Bigger Competitor Is about to Attack, You Should Attack First

Finally, you must face reality about size and force. As in war, the bigger armies generally tend to overwhelm smaller armies. More people shooting at fewer people almost always results in a victory for the side with more people.

So if you're faced with a major attack, you must find a way to attack first if for no other reason than to keep your competitor distracted and off balance. If you don't, you will be overrun quickly and decisively.

That was exactly what faced DEC as IBM was readying its small computer attack with the PC. An early launch of a more powerful, minicomputer-based desktop machine would have dramatically slowed down IBM's penetration into the business market. It would have raised questions about whether IBM's PC was powerful and serious enough. Instead, by not attacking, DEC gave IBM time to improve the power and performance of these machines by introducing new generations (the XT and the AT).

In short order, DEC's decline was set in motion.

Solution versus Direction

When problems arise, whether they are in marketing, politics, or life, everyone looks for a solution. We have all been programmed to solve problems with solutions.

Interestingly, my many years of being in the problem-solving business have led me to believe that often looking for a solution is a fool's errand. There is no easy solution for complex problems. What there is instead is an obvious direction. The reason is that often there are too many variables in a situation. Unlike solving a mathematical problem, you are often dealing with the human condition, which certainly adds a level of complexity that would drive a mathematician to drink. There's competition or personal agendas or disruptive technology or, in diplomacy, country interest.

A longer-term direction is a lot more flexible because it gives you some maneuvering room to deal with change and unpredictable events. Often just knowing where you are going is the best you can do in a difficult situation. It also is the essence of a good strategy.

Let me explain this process in two examples. One is a business problem and the other is a diplomatic problem. Both are very complex and very serious. And both are very similar.

The first is General Motors (GM). As you've read, there is no easy solution for a company that has steadily lost market share for over 20 years. The result: too many plants, too many people, too many retirees with high health-care costs, and brands that have lost their meaning with years of making them look alike, sound alike, and pricing alike. This situation can only be resolved with a change of direction and that direction is obvious. GM has to reposition all its brands so that the marketplace will know the difference between Saturn, Chevrolet, Pontiac, Buick, and Cadillac. In other words, if BMW stands for driving, Mercedes stands for prestige, and Toyota stands for reliability, what do GM's brands stand for? In many ways, it is what Alfred Sloan did when he put GM on a successful run to achieving almost half of the U.S. car market. (More on this in Chapter 9.)

Getting this done won't be easy because each brand must be given a unique position, styling, and pricing and then each must stand on its own. In other words, we're talking about major surgery and, if necessary, cutting out a brand that has no natural place to go in a world of killer competition. Doing this in the short term will not be possible. It will be a long, step-by-step journey. But at least they will know where they are going. It is a clear direction.

The second example is the mother of all problems. It's called Iraq. You might say that Iraq isn't a marketing problem. I beg to differ. To me this is a gigantic selling problem to the U.S. public, to the world community, and to the Iraqis. But there is no easy solution to sell, which is why President Bush has had so much trouble selling his ideas. Every so-called "solution" has failed or has been picked apart. It's time to try selling a "direction."

Like GM, Iraq has a multitude of brands: The Kurds, the Sunnis, and the Shiites. And, again like GM, the current attempt is to force them to put their differences aside and form a unified government where they all look alike and sound alike. It's apparent that this "solution" isn't working because these brands don't trust each other and, if you read history, they never will.

So what's called for is a direction that accommodates this basic fact of life in Iraq. What makes sense is, again like GM, to let brands run independently. That means three states with their own security and legislation. The only role for a federal government is to find a way to divide up the resources (oil revenue) so that each brand can build a degree of prosperity for their people. And prosperity is our best weapon against terrorism. Why? Because people quickly realize that terrorism is bad for business.

Would people in the United States buy this strategy? Absolutely. Would Iraq's neighbors buy in? Absolutely. Will the world community think it's a good direction? No doubt. And, with an oil-sharing program, the Iraqis would most likely buy into this direction.

The toughest sell will be the Bush administration that has been marketing a unified country as an example of freedom and democracy in the Middle East.

But, hey, what do I know, I'm only a marketing guy trying to encourage good directions instead of just solutions.

Mission Statement Words

An obvious marketing strategy is like a mission statement and you could assume that once a company understands its basic differentiating strategy, it would be a simple matter to sit down and fold it into such a statement.

Don't make that assumption.

Since Volvo is all about safety, its obvious mission statement would read something like: "Volvo is in business to make the safest vehicles in the world."

Do you think Volvo has anything like that hanging on its walls? Nope. It has a mission statement of 130 words and "safety" shows up as the 126th word. (It barely made it into the statement.)

It's no wonder that Volvo is drifting into hot, sporty models—convertibles like its C70. On these cars, gone is that safe "tanky" look. If it keeps this up, gone will be its business as well.

It is current thinking that a mission statement helps define what a company wants to be when it grows up. Companies spend weeks and months agonizing over every word.

If you explore this thinking, you'll see there is a widely accepted process for creating these statements. The following chart presents the phases of effort along with our remarks about the problems that we see with each phase.

How Mission Statements Are Born

Phase 1: Envision the future.

(It can't be done.)

Phase 2: Form a mission task force.

(Waste the time of expensive people.)

Phase 3: Develop a draft statement.

(Many hands make things mushy.)

Phase 4: Communicate the final statement.

(Hang it on the wall for people to ignore.)

Phase 5: Operationalize the statement.

(Turn the company into mush.)

As far as I'm concerned, this process adds needless complication to most companies and very little benefit.

Nothing proves this point more than glancing through a book by Jeffery Abrahams, called *The Mission Statement Book*, which contains 301 corporate mission statements from top U.S. companies. In an article in *Marketing Magazine*, a gentleman named Jeremy Bullmore sat down and counted the words most frequently used by mission statement writers. It was an exercise in counting the clichés. Here's his tally from the 301 statements:

service (230)	growth (118)
customers (211)	environment (117)
quality (194)	profit (114)
value (183)	leader (104)
employees (157)	best (102)

He also discovered that many of these 301 statements are interchangeable. (Could it be that companies are knocking off other companies' mission statements?)

Boeing wrote about "a fundamental goal of achieving 20 percent average annual return on stockholder's equity."

(That's not realistic when you consider the success of Airbus. Boeing should be talking about the business, not the numbers.)

Even the government gets into the mission statement act. The Air Force had one of the best of the bunch: "To defend the United States through control and exploitation of air and space." (Kicking ass in the air is indeed what it's about.)

The CIA had almost 200 words of motherhood and mush and not one mention about its basic problem of getting it right.

As best we can see, most of these mission statements have little positive impact on a company's business. Levitz Furniture has a mission of "satisfying the needs and expectations of our customers with quality products and services." (That wonderful mission statement didn't keep it out of bankruptcy.)

Fortunately, most companies put their mission statements in gold frames and hang them in their lobbies where top managers who have their own agendas ignore them.

A simple approach is to forget about "what you want to be." Management should focus its efforts on "what you can be." It's far more productive.

This means that you have to put your basic business strategy into the statement. It should present your differentiating idea and explain how by preempting this idea you will be in a position to outflank your competition.

Boeing's mission statement should be about maintaining leadership in the commercial aircraft industry, not about return on equity.

And you don't need a committee to spend weeks writing this statement. This should be something that the CEO and his or her top people should be able to put together in a morning's work. Keep it short and simple.

The Seagram Company mission statement spills over to 10 sentences and 198 words. (You need a tumbler of good Scotch to get through it.)

After all, if a CEO needs a committee to figure out what the basic business is about, then that company needs a new CEO, not a mission statement.

The last step is not to just hang the "what we can do" state-ment on the wall. Take this basic business strategy to all the important groups in a company and make sure they under-stand it. Let them ask questions. Be candid with your answers.

And to me, that's the only purpose of a mission statement: to make sure everyone in the company gets it. In a way you're putting the "obvious" on the wall.

Leadership: A Powerful Differentiator

This is my other favorite obvious strategy. What most bewilders me in the marketing world are companies that don't exploit their leadership. Instead of "I'm lovin' it," McDonald's could be, "The world's favorite place to eat." Instead of "Connecting people," Nokia could be "The world's No. 1 cell phone."

Leadership is the most powerful way to differentiate a brand. The reason is that it's the most direct way to establish the credentials of a brand. And credentials are the collateral you put up to guarantee the performance of your brand.

Also, when you have leadership credentials, your prospect is likely to believe almost anything you say about your brand. (Because you're the leader.) Humans tend to equate "bigness" with success, status, and leadership. We give respect and admiration to the biggest.

Powerful leaders can take ownership of the word that stands for the category. You can test the validity of a leadership claim by a word association test.

If the given words are computer, copier, chocolate bar, and cola, the four most associated words are IBM, Xerox, Hershey's, and Coke.

An astute leader will go one step further to solidify its position. Heinz owns the word *ketchup*. But Heinz went on to isolate the most important ketchup attribute. "Slowest ketchup in the West" is how the company is preempting the thickness attribute. Owning the word *slow* helps Heinz maintain a 50 percent market share.

Despite all the foregoing points about the power of being the perceived leader, we continue to come across leaders who don't want to talk about their leadership. Their response about avoiding that claim to what is rightfully theirs is often the same: "We don't want to brag."

Well, a leader who doesn't brag is the best thing that can happen to its competition. When you've clawed your way to the top of the mountain, you had better plant your flag and take some pictures.

And besides, you can often find a nice way to express your leadership. One of our favorite leadership slogans does just that: "Fidelity Investments. Where 12 million investors put their trust." Another is Titleist, "The No. 1 ball in golf."

If you don't take credit for your achievement, the competitor right behind you will find a way to claim what is rightfully yours.

If you doubt this, consider the following saga.

For years, the two big beers in Brazil were Antarctica and Brahma. Antarctica was number one and Brahma was a close-behind number two.

Then Brahma started an advertising campaign claiming leadership ("Cerveza number one"). They added point-of-sale hands with the index finger symbolizing number one. But here's the surprise. When they started this, Antarctica was still the leader but no one knew it because they had not planted their flag of leadership.

When the dust settled, guess who moved into first place? You're right. Brahma is now number one. The reason: When people thought that they weren't drinking the leading beer, they quickly shifted to Brahma and what started out as an untruth became the truth.

The moral: While people love underdogs, they buy the overdogs.

But there is a happy ending to this story because Antarctica and Brahma have now merged their companies. They can now say they both are number one.

Leadership comes in many flavors, any of which can be an effective way to differentiate yourself. Here's a quick sampling of different ways to leadership:

- *Sales leadership.* The most often used strategy by leaders is pronouncing how well they sell. Toyota still has the best-selling car in America. But others can claim their own sales leadership by carefully counting in different ways. Chrysler's Dodge Caravan is the top-selling minivan. The Ford Explorer is the top sports utility vehicle. Chevrolet is the leading American car company. This approach works because people tend to buy what others buy.

- *Technology leadership.* Some companies with long histories of technological breakthroughs can use this form of leadership as a differentiator. In Austria, a rayon fiber manufacturer called Lenzing isn't the sales leader but they are the "world's leader in viscose fiber technology." They pioneered many of the industry breakthroughs in new and improved rayon. Corning is the world's leader in the science of glass.

- *Performance leadership.* Companies have products that aren't big sellers but are big performers. This can also be used as a way to separate yourself from your lesser performing competition. The famous Porsche 911 is such a car. When one rumbles by, you know it can outperform anything on the road.

Leadership is a wonderful platform from which to tell the story of how you got to be number one. As we said earlier, people will believe whatever you say if they perceive you as a leader. They figure you know more.

What makes a company strong is not the product or the service. It's the position it owns in the mind. The strength of Hertz is in its leadership position, not the quality of its rent-a-car service. It's easier to stay on top than to get there.

Can you name a company that has overturned a leader? Crest did it in toothpaste, thanks to the American Dental Association's seal of approval. (Ironically, Colgate has regained the lead with its germ-killing Total toothpaste, though recently they are neck and neck with Crest.) Duracell did it in batteries, thanks to "alkaline." Budweiser did it in beer, and Marlboro did it in cigarettes. But it rarely happens.

A survey of 25 leading brands from the year 1923 proves this point. Today, 21 of those brands are still in first place, three are in second place, and one is in fifth place.

Even changes in rank don't happen very often. If marketing were a horse race, it would be a deadly dull affair. In the 56 years since World War II, there has been only one change in position in the top three U.S. automobile companies.

In 1950, Ford Motor company moved past Chrysler Corporation into second place among U.S. automakers. Since then, the order has been General Motors, Ford, and Chrysler all the way. Monotonous, isn't it? (That is, until Toyota barged into the game.)

The "stickiness" of a marketing race, the tendency for companies or brands to remain in the same position year after year, also underscores the importance of securing a good position in the first place. Improving your position might be difficult, but once you do, it becomes relatively easy to maintain that new position.

When you do get on top, make sure the marketplace knows it. Too many companies take their leadership for granted and never exploit it. All this does is keep the door open for competition. If you get the chance, slam the door in your competition's face.

More on Leadership

Over the years, I've received some push-back on leadership as a powerful differentiator. Let's say that you're not quite sold on the fact that being the leader is not critical to success. All right, let's spend some more time on this subject.

First, let's start with the numbers. If you study categories, you will discover a simple but startling reality about market share: Your place in the market tends to be geometric. If the leader has a 40 percent share, the No. 2 brand usually has half that or a 20 percent share. No. 3 has half again or a 10 percent share and No. 4 has a 5 percent share. Believe me, over time these numbers are very accurate. This all means that No. 1 is wonderful, No. 2 can be terrific, No. 3 is threatened, and No. 4 can be fatal.

Jack Welch of General Electric fame made his reputation on this principle. He said to his people, "I want to be No. 1 or No. 2. If not, I will sell the business." What he recognized was what I call "The Law of Duality." Most markets, over time, become a two-horse race. (More on that in Chapter 8, titled "The Law of Duality.")

The bottom line supports what we have always said, "It is better to be first than to be better."

Now, let's continue to talk about why leadership is a powerful communications message. As I wrote in the *New Positioning* (my 1996 sequel to *Positioning*), the human mind tends to be insecure when it comes to purchasing things. Psychologists have outlined five basic risks that come into play, depending on what you are buying. They are:

1. *Monetary risk.* Is it worth the money?
2. *Functional risk.* Will it work as promised?
3. *Physical risk.* Is it safe to use?
4. *Social risk.* How will I look to my friends and neighbors if I buy it?
5. *Psychological risk.* How will I feel about myself for buying this product?

In other words, to most, purchasing things can be a risky business. That's why most people don't know what they want. Most people buy what they think they should have. Based on this premise, another psychologist developed a theory that can be described as "Following the herd." His point is that "we determine what is correct by finding out what other people think is correct. We view a behavior as correct in a given situation to the degree we see others performing it."

This is why leadership as a concept is a powerful communications idea. It tells people what others are buying, which makes them comfortable in their purchase. It's also why word-of-mouth is a powerful motivator because you are being told by others why they purchased a product.

Want an example of the herd effect? Consider the SUV craze in recent years. You couldn't watch television without seeing one of these vehicles driving into a jungle or through the desert or up a glacier. How many of these vehicles actually leave the highway? Less than 10 percent. Ask a person if they are about to drive their vehicle into the bushes and they will say, "What, and scratch up my $40,000 car?" When you ask them why they bought it? They will probably answer, "Hey, you never know, I might have to go into the woods some day." Want the real reason? They bought it because everyone else bought one.

The same could be said for the current MP-3 craze. It's hard not to buy an iPod after you've seen 20 or 30 people walk by with those things plugged into their ears. (What are they listening to that I'm missing?)

Finally, leadership can be expressed in many ways and you don't have to hit people over the head with your No. 1 status. Many years ago, Cadillac came out with a great way to express their leadership (At the time.) Their line: "The leader should do more. It's only right."

Nike could nail down their leadership by simply stating the obvious, "What the world's best athletes wear." (Nike should know this since they hired all the best athletes.)

There are times where your leadership is clearly understood by your customers so it doesn't have to be mentioned. As I've noted, Quiksilver, the dominant and very hip leader in surfboard and skateboard clothing probably should keep their size and dominance under wraps. Their founder said when asked about why they didn't expand into wider distribution, "Big is the enemy of cool." (Unfortunately, they are now headed into young women's casual wear. That's not a cool move.)

So, there you go. If you want to use a meaningless slogan instead of declaring your leadership, be my guest. Or, if you feel you'll find happiness as an also-ran, all I can say is good luck.

Something Borrowed Is Simpler

I picked up a recent big new idea book titled *Blue Ocean Strategy*. The basic idea in this book is about pursuing and creating new products and services (blue oceans) instead of duking it out with established competitors in existing categories (red oceans). It's an excellent book.

It is absolutely a smart way to go. In fact we have been preaching this concept for years. In my 1981 book *Positioning*, you'll find, "It's better to be first than better" and in the 1985 book *Marketing Warfare,* you'll read about, "Flanking warfare moves into uncontested areas that avoids established competitors."

Did the authors borrow old ideas and build on them? Sure. They have followed Thomas Edison's advice when he said, "Your idea needs to be original only in its adaptation to the problem you are currently working on."

The simplest way to solve a problem is to borrow an existing idea. Military designers borrowed from Picasso's art to create better camouflage pattern for tanks.

The simplest way to invent a new product is to adapt an existing idea. The pop singer and composer Paul Simon was asked where he got the inspiration for "Bridge over Troubled Water." He said he was carrying around two melodies in his head—a Bach chorale and a gospel tune from the Swan Silvertones—"and I just pieced them together." An honest reply, indeed.

The Museum of Paleontology at the University of California at Berkeley held a dinosaur body-parts sale. The museum asked contributors to sponsor parts of a Tyrannosaurus rex that had to be assembled. Donors' names would appear on a plaque at the museum. Prices ranged from $20 for a tailbone to $5,000 for the skull and jaws. (In case you're wondering, there are 300 pieces in your average T-rex skeleton.)

The effort was a huge success. People bought dinosaur parts in their kids' names. Elementary schools held bake sales to sponsor a bone.

And where did this idea come from? It was borrowed. The fund drive was akin to an opera house selling individual seats to benefactors.

You can increase your odds of solving a problem by becoming a collector. When you come across a nifty notion or a savvy strategy, save it. Start a journal, a clipping file, and a computer file. Keep a pad by the bed, a voice recorder in the car.

When you're trying to find a solution to something, dip into your collection. Then use the following blueprint to make the most of an existing idea. (The blueprint itself is adapted from a checklist by Alex Osborn, author of *Applied Imagination*.)

1. *Substitute.* What could you substitute in the approach, materials, ingredients, or appearance? Sugar Pops became Corn Pops, a more nutrition-conscious cereal. *Romeo and Juliet* begat *West Side Story*.

2. *Combine.* What could you blend with an existing idea? What ingredients, appeals, colors, flavors? Lipton combined fruits and flavors with its tea to develop new blends.

3. *Adapt.* What else is this idea like? What could you copy? Sony adapted its Walkman concept into the Watchman TV and Discman CD. (This has been called a "managed evolution" of a product or process.) Unfortunately, they missed a digital version of the Walkman that turned out to be the iPod. Big mistake.

4. *Magnify or minimize.* What if you added, lengthened, strengthened, or subtracted? When sports utility vehicles were selling like hotcakes, Ford upped the ante with the even bigger Expedition and the Lincoln Navigator. GM went for the Hummer. (Unfortunately, the SUV party is over.)

5. *Put it to other uses.* What other ways could you use what you already have? Arm & Hammer transformed baking soda into a refrigerator deodorant, an underarm deodorant, and a toothpaste ingredient. Folks in Coatesville, Pennsylvania, transformed an old boarded-up hospital into a shelter for the homeless and apartments for low-income elderly.

6. *Eliminate.* What could you get rid of? Saturn set out to eliminate the fear and loathing of salespeople in the car-buying process. The Cirque du Soleil eliminated the tents, animals, and clowns from the circus and became the kind of success that Barnum & Bailey could only dream about.

7. *Reverse or rearrange.* What could you transpose or look at backward? Reverse the physics of a cold thermos and you have a hot thermos.

8. *Shift audiences.* Is there a segment being ignored to whom you can pitch your product? Curves focused on women for their workout facilities and ignored men. Lowe's also focused their home improvement stores on women and walked away from those macho contractors. Big success in both instances.

Dale Carnegie, of *How to Win Friends and Influence People* fame, was a famous borrower. He once wrote: "The ideas I stand for are not mine. I borrowed them from Socrates. I swiped them from Chesterfield. I stole them from Jesus. And

I put them in a book. If you don't like their rules, whose would you use?"

Often floating in those Blue Oceans are borrowed ideas.

Coping in a Changing World

Not long ago, an article caught my attention. It was titled "Kodak Takes Hit in Film and Digital." It discussed, in some detail, how analysts had begun to question just what future the firm that has been synonymous with film and pictures might have in the consumer photography market. This problem is worth writing about because it is an example of what can happen to even the biggest brands in an era of change. But to learn, you must study history.

Like AT&T and GM, Kodak is an industry icon that is having difficulty dealing with competition and new technology. Because of their long history of success, they have put inordinate faith in their name and logo. They could do what they wanted to do.

A fundamental mistake that big, successful companies often make is to see themselves and their reputation far beyond the way the world is willing to see them. The corporate feeling is, "All I have to do is put my well-known name on the product and the world will buy it."

No they won't. Especially if you're horning in on someone else's specialty. And besides, the world also loves an alternative. So if you're sitting there all alone, enjoy it while you can because as soon as an attractive alternative comes along, you're going to lose some business.

During the 1870s, George Eastman, a young bank clerk in Rochester, New York, took an avid interest in photography. But wet-plate photographic equipment was bulky and unwieldy, so people could not take a camera on a trip. A photographer traveled with a photographic outfit of which the camera was only a part. After much work in his mother's sink, Eastman came up with dry plates and gelatin-coated paper "film" to be used with his new, patented roll holder. Small cameras were then possible, and at least, people could take easy-to-use cameras everywhere.

The brand name, Kodak, was another invention of Eastman. "K" happened to be Eastman's favorite letter. He also liked the name because it was short, easily pronounced, and didn't resemble any other brand name in the industry. It was and is a brilliant name.

He topped that great name with a brilliant positioning line for his advertising:

Kodak Cameras.
You press the button.
We do the rest.

The rest is history: Photography became a gigantic industry and that little yellow film box was its visual symbol. Everything went swimmingly until, you guessed it, a strong alternative arrived.

In the late 1970s, the weak Japanese yen allowed a very strong competitor to get a toehold in the U.S. market. Fuji Photo entered the fray with a little green box of film that challenged Kodak's dominance in the photographic paper market. By offering a similar quality product at a much lower price, Fuji began capturing a substantial share of the U.S. market through the 1980s and 1990s. In 1996, Kodak had an 80 percent share against Fuji's 10 percent. By the year 2000, Kodak's share was estimated at 65 percent as against Fuji's 25 percent.

The lesson Kodak missed here was that *leaders have to block.* It took too long for Kodak to aggressively reduce its prices to challenge Fuji's aggressive pricing moves. The competitive rule in play is that you always have to stay in the ballpark on pricing. Even the vaunted Marlboro brand discovered this as they dramatically dumped their price to counter low-price cigarettes. (They dumped their stock price as well.)

By hanging back and allowing a big price differential, Kodak encouraged people to discover that Fuji pictures came out about as well as Kodak pictures. And when in 1984, Kodak lost the title of "official film of the 1984 Summer Olympics" to Fuji, it solidified the perception of Fuji being a legitimate alternative and not just a low-price brand.

Green was here to stay as the alternative to yellow.

Having to cope with Fuji was one thing, but having to cope with the arrival of digital pictures just might be Kodak's ultimate test of survival. To succeed in their next century of existence, they will likely have to shift toward newer digital imaging technologies that will be a far cry from Mother Eastman's sink. Kodak faces fierce competition from U.S. and Japanese companies like Hewlett-Packard, Sony, and Canon that are accustomed to the quick pace of change in digital technology. Many believe that Kodak's chances of making a profit with digital camera manufacturing are slim. Most analysts feel that Kodak will ultimately fail to reinvent itself and make it into the ranks of leading U.S. digital corporations.

I agree with that, especially if you're talking about the Kodak brand.

As I've often written, *if you're known for one thing, the market will not give you another thing.* Kodak is "film" in the minds of the marketplace and not "camera." Nikon, which is a camera in our minds, has a better chance at becoming a successful digital camera (the latest form of camera).

If you view the new camera as "electronic," Canon, Sony, and Hewlett-Packard have a better chance at being big in digital picture systems.

Because each emerging market segment has its own leader, Kodak, the leader in film photographic technology, has little chance of becoming the leader in the segment of digital photographic technology once the category is underway and has momentum.

Kodak's best chance would have been to buy or launch a new brand in this arena some years ago. Ironically, a scientist at Kodak actually invented digital photography. That invention should have been nurtured despite its potential to undermine the film business. It's better to attack yourself than to have a competitor do it.

The Kodak brand would be reserved for film. The new brand or company would have no Kodak connection and would run on its own. Kodak's headquarters would be in Rochester, New York. The new company would be headquartered as far away as possible, say, somewhere in Silicon Valley.

This type of move would have been hard for Kodak to swallow since it attacked the mother lode. But, if they continue to try to turn their 100-year-old film brand into a nonfilm brand, the future picture doesn't look very sharp.

Big Is the Enemy of Obvious

Two articles about conglomerates appeared that struck a déjà vu all over again chord. The first was about General Electric being not very happy about their stock price and the fact that their plastics business was on the block. The other article was about Citigroup's stock price problems as they lag behind the performance of the likes of Goldman Sachs and JPMorgan Chase.

The Citigroup article questioned the conglomerate model and pointed out the loss of the talent needed to run the different kinds of businesses that Sandy Weill has assembled: global consumer finance, wealth management, investment banking, and corporate lending.

Some years ago, I wrote a book titled *Big Brands. Big Trouble*. One chapter was titled, "The Bigger They Are, the Harder to Manage."

When you start to study the subject of getting big, you can quickly come up with a stunning amount of research and analysis that seriously questions whether bigger is better. By the time I was finished, I began to wonder what in the world these CEOs were thinking about as they got trapped in the land of mergermania.

In a detailed study, two economists produced a 400-page analysis that confronts the quintessential myth of corporate culture: that industrial giants in an organizational bigness are the handmaidens of economic efficiency. In a 1986 book titled, The *Bigness Complex*, they argue that the preoccupation with bigness is at the heart of the U.S. economic decline.

A little hindsight shows that they miscalled our "economic decline." Quite the opposite occurred as we roared off into an amazing economic expansion. They also missed that these big companies have been falling apart on their own and we don't need any government policy to keep bad bigness things from happening. And they missed the small company explosion in high-tech land that helped propel our expansion.

After an intense amount of original and observed research, the authors concluded that conglomerate bigness seldom enhances, and more typically undermines, efficiency in production.

It's no wonder that big business has been replacing huge manufacturing complexes with new, smaller plants. Companies discovered that their people can't manage their way out of the problems created by size and complexity.

Economists do touch on the difficulties of organizing big companies, but to me, the best analysis of managing size came from a British anthropologist named Robin Dunbar. In an excellent book titled *The Tipping Point,* Malcolm Gladwell introduces us to Dunbar, whose work revolved around what he called *social capacity:* how big a group we can run with and feel comfortable. His observation is that humans socialize in the largest group of primates because we are the only animals with brains large enough to handle the complexities of that social arrangement. His observation was that the figure of 150 seems to have a genuinely social relationship that goes with knowing who they are and how they relate to us.

Mr. Gladwell extracted from Dunbar's work the following observation that gets to the heart of being too big:

> At a bigger size you have to impose complicated hierarchies and rules and regulations and formal measures to try to command loyalty and cohesion. But below 150, Dunbar argues, it is possible to achieve these same goals informally: "At this size orders can be implemented and unruly behavior controlled on the basis of personal loyalties and direct man-to-man contacts. With larger groups, this becomes impossible." (p. 180)

Betting big by merger can also be big trouble.

At the turn of the twentieth century, a great number of corporate giants were created: General Electric (a combination of 8 firms controlling 90 percent of the market); Du Pont (64 firms controlling 70 percent); Nabisco (27 firms, 70 percent); Otis Elevator (6 firms, 65 percent); International Paper (24 firms, 60 percent).

But those good old days are over. The past 30 years are strewn with failures: the 1970s conglomerates often failed to produce promised profits and the 1980s buyouts often reduced efficiency and saddled companies with more debt than they could repay. And merging distinct corporations sometimes takes longer than expected which only gives our friends on Wall Street high anxiety. They call it a clash of corporate cultures.

Let me end with a personal story about "big." Many years ago, I started my marketing career at General Electric. One of my first marketing problems was trying to launch the "turnkey power plant." The concept was to sell the utility the entire plant since only GE made all the components. It never flew. The utility wanted to put the pieces together themselves and select the components they thought were best.

Next up was the "GE kitchen." The strategy was to go to the lady of the house with all the necessary appliances since only GE made them all. It never flew. The lady wanted to put the kitchen together herself and select the appliances she thought were best.

Two lessons learned.

Both lessons pointed to the underlying problem of being too big. Your customers just won't be impressed. They want the best of the breed and everything for everybody isn't much of an argument. In fact, it's the opposite. Common sense tells customers that you can't be the best at everything.

Game over, big guys.

Major Marketing Mistakes

In today's world, there's so much competition that if you make a mistake your competitors quickly get your business. The chances of getting it back are very slim unless someone else makes a mistake. Hoping competitors make mistakes is like running a race hoping the other racers fall down: It just doesn't happen very often.

Here are the obvious blunders that are the most prevalent in today's hypercompetitive world:

- *Me-Too.* Many people believe that the basic issue in marketing is convincing prospects that you have a better product or service. They say to themselves, "We might not be first, but we're going to be better." That might be true, but if you're late, and you have to do battle with large, well-established competitors, then your marketing strategy is probably faulty. Me-too just won't cut it.

- *What are you selling?* This may surprise you, but a good bit of my time over the years has been spent figuring out exactly what it is that people are trying to sell. In other words, trying to capture the category in a simple, understandable way. Companies, large and small, often have a very tough time describing their product, especially if it's a new category and a new technology. Your biggest marketing successes come with simple, but powerful explanations of what you're offering. Don't get cute or complex.

- *Truth will win out.* Not understanding that marketing is a battle of perceptions is a simple truth that trips up thousands of would-be entrepreneurs every year. Marketing people are preoccupied with doing research and "getting the facts." They analyze the situation to make sure the truth is on their side.

  Then they sail confidently into the marketing arena, secure in the knowledge that they have the best product and that ultimately the best product will win. It's an illusion. There is no objective reality. There are no facts. There are no best products. All that exists in the world of marketing are perceptions in the minds of the customer or prospect. The perception is the reality. Everything else is an illusion.

- *The other person's idea.* It's bad enough to launch a me-too product, but equally problematic is a me-too idea. The reason is that two companies cannot own the same concept in the prospect's mind. When a competitor owns a word or position in the prospect's mind, it is futile to attempt to own the same word. Toyota has preempted the concept of "reliability." Many other automobile companies, including Mercedes-Benz and General Motors have tried to run marketing campaigns based on reliability. Yet, no one except Toyota has succeeded in getting into the prospect's mind with a reliability message.

- *We're very successful.* As I've written in the past, success often leads to arrogance and arrogance to failure. When people become successful, they tend to become less objective. They often substitute their own judgment for what the market wants.

  As their successes mounted, companies like General Motors, Sears, and IBM became arrogant. They felt they could do anything they wanted to in the marketplace. Success leads to trouble.

- *Everything for everybody.* When you try to be all things to all people, you inevitably wind up in trouble. Better advice comes from one manager who said, "I'd rather be strong somewhere than weak everywhere." This kind of "all things" thinking leads to what we call "line extension," or trying to use a successful brand to mean more than it can in the mind. It's a very popular mistake.

- *Live by the numbers.* Big companies are in a bind. On the one hand, they have Wall Street asking, "How much are your sales and profits going to grow next month, next quarter, next year?" On the other hand, there are an endless number of competitors saying, "We're not going to let you grow if we can help it."

  So what happens? The CEO lies to Wall Street and then turns around to the marketing people and tells them what is expected in terms of profit and growth. They in turn scramble back to their offices and try to figure out how to make those unreasonable numbers. Brash predictions about earnings growth often lead to missed targets, battered stock, and even creative accounting. But worse than that, it leads to bad decisions.

  As panic sets in, what often happens is that they fall into the line extension, or the everything-for-everybody trap. Rather than staying focused on being strong somewhere, to drive their numbers up, they opt for being weak everywhere. Their only hope is that they will be promoted before it all hits the fan.

- *Not attacking yourself.* Much has been written about the likes of DEC, Xerox, AT&T, and Kodak, and their efforts to move from slow growth to high growth businesses. When this is exacerbated, companies are faced with what have been called *disruptive technologies*. DEC facing the desktop computer revolution. Xerox facing the surge in laser printing, and Kodak facing the digital camera.

Though difficult, a leader has no choice in this matter. They must find a way to move to that better idea or technology, even if it threatens their base business. If they don't, their future will be in question. Especially as that technology is improved and picks up momentum. The trick is how to do it.

CHAPTER

8

You Must Be Aware of Some Obvious Ground Rules

In another book, I wrote about the laws of marketing. A number of these are very important in the search for the obvious. Ignore them at your own risk.

Law of the Ear

Your obvious strategy has to sound right if it is to explode in people's minds.

Has anyone ever asked you which is more powerful, the eye or the ear? Probably not, because the answer is obvious. I'll bet that deep down you believe the eye is more powerful than the ear. Call it *visual chauvinism*, if you like, but it's a preconception held by many marketing people.

I'll bet, too, that you share a related preconception, first expressed some 500 years before the birth of Christ: Confucius said, "A picture is worth a thousand words."

Those seven words—not *pictures*, mind you, but *words*—
have lived for 2,500 years. And the way things have been
going lately, it seems like those seven words will never die.
What agency president, creative director, or art director
hasn't quoted Confucius at least once in his or her career?

After analyzing hundreds of effective positioning programs,
we ran into a surprising conclusion: The programs were all
verbal. There wasn't a single positioning concept that was
exclusively visual. Could Confucius have been wrong? We
have come to the conclusion that the mind works by ear, not
by eye. A picture is *not* worth a thousand words.

If you looked at just the pictures in almost any magazine or
newspaper, you would learn very little. If you read just the
words, however, you would have a pretty good idea of what
was said.

In spite of the evidence all around us, communications people suffer from "wordophobia," a morbid fear of words. In
order to set the record straight, we attempted to find out
exactly what Confucius said. We took the Chinese characters
and had them translated. Confucius said: "A picture is worth a
thousand pieces of gold." Not *words*, but *gold!*

We knew instantly that here was a true prophet. What Confucius foresaw was television and the movies, where a picture
does indeed sell for thousands of pieces of gold. Son of a gun!
And here, all these years, I thought he was knocking *words!*

But what is a *picture* worth on television? That is, *just* the
picture, without the sound?

Not much. As a matter of fact, without the words on the
package or the graphics on the screen, pictures in a TV commercial have almost no communication value. But add sound
(words), and the "picture" changes.

If pictures alone make no sense, how about sound alone?
Strange as it may seem, sound alone in a television commercial

usually carries an easy-to-understand message. Most classic print advertisements illustrate the same principle. The visual alone makes almost no sense. Naturally, a print ad with *both* pictures and words is more effective than either the words or the picture alone. But which is more powerful individually, the verbal or the visual?

Take the classic "Pepsi-Cola hits the spot" radio commercial, which first ran more than 60 years ago. Nothing, absolutely nothing, went into the mind via the eye. Yet, the commercial hit a hot spot. Even today some people can recall the opening bits of Pepsi music, and are able to recite every word of the jingle. Fifty-six years later!

That's interesting. An idea deeply embedded in the mind that didn't come in through the eyes. Something seems wrong with the conventional wisdom as to the superiority of the eye.

To obtain a more objective viewpoint on the subject, we went to an expert, the author of the authoritative book on the subject of memory. Dr. Elizabeth Loftus of the University of Washington is a psychologist, teacher, researcher, and author of more than eight books and 100 articles on the human mind and how it works. When we asked her which is superior, the eye or the ear, this was her reply:

> In many ways, the ear is superior to the eye. What I mean by that is that there is evidence from controlled laboratory studies that shows that when you present a list of words to people, and you present it either auditorily, say on a tape recorder, or you present it visually, say on slides, people remember more words if they hear the words than if they see them.

In *Positioning: The Battle for Your Mind*, we said: "The name is the hook that hangs the brand on the product ladder in the prospect's mind." Now we know *why*. Apparently, thinking itself involves the manipulation of sounds deep inside the brain—even when the stimulus is purely visual, as with printed words.

Shakespeare was wrong: A rose by any other name would *not* smell as sweet. Not only do you see what you want to see, you also smell what you want to smell. Which is why the single most important decision in the marketing of a perfume is the name you decide to put on the brand.

Would "Alfred" perfume have sold as well as "Charlie"? We doubt it. And Hog Island in the Caribbean was going nowhere until its name was changed to Paradise Island.

"Language and writing," said Ferdinand de Saussure, a famous Belgian linguist, "are two distinct systems of signs. The second exists for the sole purpose of representing the first." Translation: Print is a secondary medium that exists as a representation of the primary medium of sound.

The implications of these findings for the advertising industry are staggering. In many ways, they call for a complete reorientation from the visual to the verbal point of view. This isn't to say that the visual doesn't play an important role. Of course it does. But the verbal should be the driver, while the pictures reinforce the words. All too often the opposite is the case.

First off, then, the printed words should carry the sales message. Cute or confusing words bring nothing but trouble.

Second, headlines should *sound* good, as well as look good. The rhyme or rhythm of the words can be powerful memory devices.

Finally, pictures need a very quick explanation; otherwise, they will distract readers. "Stopping" people won't accomplish much, if they look but don't read.

In a television commercial, spoken words should carry the sales message. Most important, you should never let the pictures and movements overwhelm the sound. When this happens, viewers stop listening and little communication takes place.

This *distraction factor* explains why so many commercials tend to be misidentified by the public. It also explains why Procter & Gamble's much-maligned slice-of-life approach works so well. The format is verbally driven and rarely contains any visual distraction. People don't rave about these commercials, they just *remember* them.

Law of Division

For the first time in decades, soft drink sales volume is either flat or declining. Consumer demand for bottled water, sports drinks, and energy drinks is exploding and contributing to eroding sales. Even milk has done better than soda.

What's going on here? Well, the Law of Division has struck again. To those of you that haven't read about the tenth Immutable Law in my book *The 22 Immutable Laws*, it goes like this: *Over time, a category will divide and become two or more categories.*

Like an amoeba dividing in a petri dish, the marketing arena can be viewed as an ever-expanding sea of categories.

A category starts off as a single entity—computers, for example. But over time, the category breaks up into other segments—mainframes, minicomputers, workstations, personal computers, laptops, notebooks, pen computers.

Like the computer, the automobile started off as a single category. Three brands (Chevrolet, Ford, and Plymouth) dominated the market. Then the category divided. Today, we have luxury cars, moderately priced cars, and inexpensive cars; full-size, intermediates, and compacts; sports cars, four-wheel-drive vehicles, recreational vehicles, and minivans.

In the television industry, ABC, CBS, and NBC once accounted for 90 percent of the viewing audience. Now we have network, independent, cable, pay, and public television, and soon we'll have online television.

Beer started the same way. Today, we have imported and domestic beer; premium and popular priced beers; light, draft, and dry beers; draft beers and even nonalcoholic beer.

The Law of Division even affects countries. (Witness the mess in Yugoslavia.) In 1776, there were about 35 empires, kingdoms, and countries in the world. By World War II, the number had doubled. By 1970, there were more than 130 countries. Today, around 200 countries are generally recognized as sovereign nations. (The last time I counted.)

Each segment is a separate, distinct entity. Each segment has its own reason for existence. And each segment has its own leader, which is rarely the same as the leader of the original category.

Instead of understanding this concept of division, many corporate leaders hold the naïve belief that categories are combining. *Convergence, synergy,* and its kissing cousin the *corporate alliance* are the buzzwords in the boardrooms of America. Some years ago, the *New York Times* wrote that IBM is poised "to take advantage of the coming convergence of whole industries, including television, music, publishing, and computing."

It didn't happen. Categories are dividing, not combining.

Also, look at the much-touted category called "financial services." In the future, according to the press, we won't have banks, insurance companies, stockbrokers, or mortgage lenders. We'll have financial services companies. It never happened.

The way for the leader to maintain its dominance is to address each emerging category with a different brand name, as General Motors did in the early days with Chevrolet, Pontiac, Oldsmobile, Buick, and Cadillac.

Companies make a mistake when they try to take a well-known brand name in one category and use the same brand name in another category. A classic example is the fate that befell Volkswagen, the company that introduced the small-car category to America. Its Beetle was a big winner that grabbed 67 percent of the imported-car market in the United States.

Volkswagen was so successful that it began to think it could be like General Motors and sell bigger, faster, and sportier cars. So it swept up whatever models it was making in Germany and shipped them all to the United States. But unlike General Motors, it used the same brand, Volkswagen, for all of its models. Needless to say, the only thing that kept selling was the "small" thing, the Beetle.

Well, Volkswagen found a way to fix that. It stopped selling the Beetle in the United States and started selling a new family of big, fast, expensive Volkswagens. Now you had the Sirocco, the Jetta, the Golf GL, and the Cabriolet. It even built a plant in Pennsylvania to build these wondrous new cars.

Unfortunately for Volkswagen, the small-car category continued to expand. And since people couldn't buy a long-lasting, economical VW, they shifted to Toyota, Honda, and Nissan. Today, Volkswagen's 67 percent share has shrunk to less than 6 percent. Eventually, VW brought back the Beetle but the damage had been done.

What keeps leaders from launching a different brand to cover a new category is the fear of what will happen to their existing brands. General Motors was slow to react to the super premium category that Mercedes-Benz and BMW established. One reason was that a new brand on top of Cadillac would enrage General Motor's Cadillac dealers.

Eventually, General Motors tried to take Cadillac up-market with the $54,000 Allante. It bombed. Why would anyone spend that kind of money on a so-called Cadillac, since their neighbors would probably think they paid only $30,000 or so? No prestige.

A more obvious strategy for General Motors might have been to put a new brand into the Mercedes market. (They might have brought back the classic LaSalle brand.)

Timing is also important. You can be too early to exploit a new category. Back in the 1950s, the Nash Rambler was America's first small car. But American Motors didn't have either the courage or the money to hang in there long enough for the category to develop. As you read earlier, timeliness is important in the search for the obvious and patience is necessary if your idea is a little early.

It's better to be early than late. You can't get into the prospect's mind first unless you're prepared to spend some time waiting for things to develop.

Law of Perception

You may have noticed that the famous Six Sigma management technique came into question as Bob Nardelli was blown out of Home Depot. He had left General Electric where Jack Welch made this quality-boosting methodology famous and applied it to Home Depot with a vengeance. It didn't seem to help things as their competitor, Lowe's, nailed them with the simple but powerful concept of "Improving home improvement." They brought this to life with neater stores, no messy contractor business, and playing to the lady of the house.

This is a vivid lesson in the simple fact that a quality program is not a differentiating idea. It's not what marketing is about. Previously, I wrote about the Law of Division. This is about the Law of Perception. Marketing is not a battle of products, it's a battle of perceptions.

However, many people think marketing is a battle of products. In the long run, they figure, the best product will win. Thus, Mr. Nardelli's Six Sigma push.

Marketing people are preoccupied with doing research and "getting the facts." They analyze the situation to make sure that truth is on their side. Then they sail confidently into the marketing arena, secure in the knowledge that they have the best product and that ultimately the best product will win.

It's an illusion. There is no objective reality. There are no facts. There are no best products. All that exists in the world of marketing are perceptions in the minds of the customer or prospect. The perception is the reality. Everything else is an illusion. This is why Robert Updegraff, the gentleman I introduced you to in Chapter 1, talked about obvious ideas exploding in the mind.

All truth is relative—relative to your mind or the mind of another human being. When you say, "I'm right and the next person is wrong," all you're really saying is that you're a better perceiver than someone else.

Most people think they are better perceivers than others. They have a sense of personal infallibility. Their perceptions are always more accurate than those of their neighbors or friends. Truth and perception become fused in the mind, leaving no difference between the two.

To cope with the terrifying reality of being alone in the universe, people project themselves on the outside world. They "live" in the arena of books, movies, television, newspapers, magazines, and the Internet. They "belong" to clubs, organizations, and institutions. These outside representations of the world seem more real than the reality inside their own minds.

People cling firmly to the belief that reality is the world outside of the mind and that the individual is one small speck on a global spaceship. Actually, it's the opposite. The only reality you can be sure about is in your own perceptions. If the universe exists, it exists inside your own mind and the minds of others. That's the reality that marketing programs must deal with. Most marketing mistakes stem from the assumption that you're fighting a product battle rooted in reality.

What some marketing people see as the natural laws of marketing are based on a flawed premise that the product is the hero of the marketing program and that you'll win or lose based on the merits of the product. Which is why the natural, logical way to market a product is invariably wrong. Only by studying how perceptions are formed in the mind and focusing your marketing programs on those perceptions can you overcome your basically incorrect marketing instincts.

Each of us (manufacturer, distributor, dealer, prospect, customer) looks at the world through a pair of eyes. If there is objective truth out there, how would we know it? Who would measure it? Who would tell us? It could only be another person looking at the same scene through a different pair of eyes—windows.

Truth is nothing more or less than one expert's perception. And who is the expert? It's someone who is perceived to be an expert in the mind of somebody else.

If the truth is so illusive, why is there so much discussion in marketing about the so-called facts? Why are so many marketing decisions based on factual comparisons? Why do so many marketing people assume that truth is on their side, that their job is to use truth as a weapon to correct the misperceptions that exist in the mind of the prospect?

Marketing people focus on facts because they believe in objective reality. It's also easy for marketing people to assume

that truth is on their side. If you think you need the best product to win a marketing battle, then it's easy to believe you
have the best product. All that's required is a minor modifica-
tion of your own perceptions.

Changing a prospect's mind is another matter. Minds of
customers or prospects are very difficult to change. With a
modicum of experience in a product category, a consumer
assumes that he or she is right. A perception that exists in the
mind is often interpreted as a universal truth. People are seldom, if ever, wrong—at least in their own minds.

It's easier to see the power of perception over product when
the products are separated by some distance. For example, the
three largest-selling Japanese imported cars in America are
Toyota, Honda, and Nissan. Most marketing people think the
battle between the three brands is based on quality, styling,
horsepower, and price. Not true. It's what people *think* about a
Toyota, a Honda, or a Nissan that determines which brand
will win. Marketing is a battle of perceptions.

Japanese automobile manufacturers sell the same cars in the
United States as they do in Japan. If marketing were a battle
of products, you would think the same sales order would hold
true for both countries. After all, the same quality, the same
styling, the same horsepower, and roughly the same prices
hold true for Japan as they do for the United States. But in
Japan, Honda is nowhere near the leader. There, Honda is in
third place, behind Toyota and Nissan. Toyota sells more
than four times as many automobiles in Japan as Honda does.

So what's the difference between Honda in Japan and
Honda in the United States? The products are the same, but
the perceptions in customers' minds are different.

If you told friends in New York you bought a Honda, they
might ask you, "What kind of Honda did you get? A Civic?
An Accord?" If you told friends in Tokyo you bought a

Honda, they might ask you, "What kind of motorcycle did you buy?" In Japan, Honda got into customers' minds as a manufacturer of motorcycles, and apparently most people don't want to buy a car from a motorcycle company.

Think about this: Would Harley-Davidson be successful if it launched a Harley-Davidson automobile? You might think it would depend on the car's quality, styling, horsepower, pricing. You might even believe the Harley-Davidson reputation for quality would be a plus. We think not. Its perception as a motorcycle company would undermine a Harley-Davidson car—no matter how good the product. (That's the Law of Line Extension.)

Some soft-drink executives believe that marketing is a battle of taste. Well, New Coke was No. 1 in taste. (The Coca-Cola Company conducted 200,000 taste tests that "proved" that New Coke tastes better than Pepsi-Cola and Pepsi tastes better than Coke's original formula, now called Coca-Cola Classic.) But who is winning the marketing battle? The drink that research had proven to taste the best, New Coke, is no longer with us. The one that research shows tasted the worst, Coca-Cola Classic, is in first place.

You believe what you want to believe. You taste what you want to taste. Soft-drink marketing is a battle of perceptions, not a battle of taste.

What makes the battle even more difficult is that customers frequently make buying decisions based on second-hand perceptions. Instead of using their own perceptions, they base their buying decisions on someone else's perception of reality. This is the "everybody knows" principle.

Everybody knows that the Japanese make higher-quality cars than the Americans do. So people make buying decisions based on the fact that everybody knows the Japanese make higher-quality cars. When you ask shoppers whether they have had any personal experience with a product, most often they say they haven't. And, more often than not, their own experience is twisted to conform to their perceptions.

If you have had a bad experience with a Japanese car, you've just been unlucky because everybody knows the Japanese make high-quality cars. Conversely, if you have had a good experience with an American car, you've just been lucky because everybody knows that American cars are not as well made.

Marketing is not a battle of products. It's a battle of perceptions. Unfortunately, Mr. Nardelli never quite understood this law.

Law of Singularity

In your search for the obvious, only one move will produce substantial results. You do not have the luxury of picking from a selection of ideas.

Many marketing people see success as the sum total of a lot of small efforts beautifully executed.

They think they can pick and choose from a number of different strategies and still be successful as long as they put enough effort into the program. If they work for the leader in the category, they fritter away their resources on a number of different programs. They seem to think that the best way to grow is the puppy approach—get into everything.

If they're not with the leader, they often end up trying to do the same as the leader, but a little better. It was like Saddam Hussein saying that all we have to do is fight a little harder and everything will work out. Trying harder is not the secret of marketing success.

Whether you try hard or not, the differences are marginal. Furthermore, the bigger the company, the more the Law of

Averages wipes out any real advantage of a trying-harder approach.

History teaches that the only thing that works in marketing is the single, bold stroke. Furthermore, in any given situation, there is only one move that will produce substantial results.

Successful generals study the battleground and look for that one bold stroke that is least expected by the enemy. Finding one is difficult. Finding more than one is usually impossible.

Military strategist and author B. H. Liddell Hart calls this bold stroke "the line of least expectation." The Allied invasion came at Normandy, a place whose tide and rocky shore the Germans felt would be an unlikely choice for a landing of any scale.

So it is in marketing. Most often, there is only one place where a competitor is vulnerable. And that place should be the focus of the entire invading force.

The automobile industry is an interesting case in point. For years, the leader's main strength was in the middle of the line. With brands like Chevrolet, Pontiac, Oldsmobile, Buick, and Cadillac, General Motors easily beat back frontal assaults by Ford, Chrysler, and American Motors. (The Edsel fiasco is a typical example.) General Motors's dominance became legendary.

What works in marketing is the same as what works in the military: the unexpected.

Hannibal came over the Alps, a route deemed impossible. Hitler came around the Maginot Line and sent his panzer divisions through the Ardennes, terrain the French generals thought impossible to traverse with tanks. (As a matter of fact, he did it twice—once in the Battle of France and again in the Battle of the Bulge.)

In recent decades, there have been only two strong moves made against General Motors. Both were flanking moves around the GM Maginot Line. The Japanese came at the low end with small cars like Toyota, Datsun, and Honda. The Germans came at the high end with super premium cars like Mercedes and BMW.

With the success of these flanking attacks, General Motors was under pressure to commit resources in an attempt to shore up the bottom and the top of its lines. (As mentioned, Cadillacs were too cheap to block the high-priced German imports.)

In an effort to save money and maintain profits, General Motors made the fateful decision to build many of its mid-range cars using the same body style. Suddenly, no one could tell a Chevrolet from a Pontiac or an Oldsmobile or a Buick. They all looked alike. (More on this in Chapter 9.)

Its look-alike cars weakened General Motors in the middle and opened up a move for Ford as it broke through with the European-styled Taurus and Sable. And then the Japanese jumped in with Toyota, Lexus, and Acura. Now General Motors is weak across the board.

Let's go back to Coke. We have seen endless slogans or ideas for Coca-Cola: "We have a taste for you," "The real choice," "Catch the wave," "Red, white and you," "You can't beat the feeling," and "The Coke side of life."

What Coke never realized was that the only obvious idea they had was the "Real Thing" and they should have used it against Pepsi's only obvious idea, the youth-oriented "Pepsi Generation."

To pull the trigger, Coke should have gone on television and said to the Pepsi Generation, "All right kids, we're not going to push you. When you're ready for the Real Thing, we've got it for you." That would be the beginning of the end of the Pepsi Generation (if Pepsi-Cola hadn't already killed it off all by itself).

Not only is this idea obvious and powerful, but it was really the only move available to Coke. It exploited the only words that Coke owns in the minds of its prospects: *The Real Thing*.

To find that singular idea or concepts, marketing managers have to know what's happening in the marketplace. They have to be down at the frontlines. They have to know what's working and what isn't. They have to be involved.

Because of the high cost of mistakes, management can't afford to delegate important marketing decisions. That's what happened at General Motors. When the financial people took over, the marketing programs collapsed. Their interest was in the numbers, not the brands. The irony is that the numbers went south, along with the brands.

It's hard to find that single obvious move if you're hanging around headquarters and not involved in the process.

Law of Duality

Microsoft just bet $44.6 billion on the Law of Duality. For those not familiar with this law, it goes like this: In the long run, every market becomes a two-horse race.

At the moment, Google has a 54 percent share of the search engine business. Yahoo is at 20 percent and Microsoft is at 13 percent. If Microsoft succeeds in acquiring Yahoo, their share jumps to 33 percent and there are two horses running after the online advertising business. (So far, this merger is up in the air. We'll have to wait on that number.) What makes this bet tricky is the fact that Google has become a generic brand. That's when a brand is used generically in everyday language, "Google his name." or "I'll Google it." The brand is both a noun and a verb at the same time. "Scotch tape it." Or "Xerox it." When this happens you can have an enormous advantage over the competition. While it drives lawyers crazy because of their fear of losing a trademark, it is the grand slam of marketing. Viagra is already a generic brand. Their share is 60 percent of the market. Cialis is at 27 percent. Levitra is at 13 percent. The Law of Duality has already struck.

Early on, a new category is a ladder of many rungs. Gradually, the ladder becomes a two-rung affair.

In batteries, it's Eveready and Duracell. In photographic film, it's Kodak and Fuji. In mouthwash, it's Listerine and Scope. In hamburgers, it's McDonald's and Burger King. In sneakers, it's Nike and Reebok. In toothpaste, it's Crest and Colgate.

When you take the long view of marketing, you find the battle usually winds up as a titanic struggle between two major players—usually the old reliable brand and the upstart. A little history is in order.

Back in 1969, there were three major brands of a certain product. The leader had about 60 percent of the market, the No. 2 brand had a 25 percent share, and the No. 3 brand had a 6 percent share. The rest of the market included either private label or minor brands. The Law of Duality suggests that these market shares are unstable. Furthermore, the law predicts that the leader will lose market share and No. 2 will gain.

Today, the leader dropped down to 43 percent of the market. The No. 2 brand has 31 percent, and No. 3 doesn't make the charts. The products are Coca-Cola, Pepsi-Cola, and Royal Crown cola, respectively, but the principles apply to brands everywhere. Look what happened to Royal Crown cola. Back in 1969, the Royal Crown company revitalized its franchise system, 350 bottlers strong, and hired the former president of Rival Pet Foods and a veteran of both Coke and Pepsi. The company also retained Wells, Rich, Greene, a high-powered New York advertising agency. "We're out to kill Coke and Pepsi," declared Mary Wells Lawrence, the agency's head, to the Royal Crown bottlers. "I hope you'll excuse the word, but we're really out for the jugular." The only brand that got killed was Royal Crown. In a maturing industry, third place is a difficult position to be in.

Take the domestic automobile industry. In spite of heroic measures undertaken by Lee Iacocca and others, Chrysler is in big trouble. In the long run, marketing is a two-horse race. Today, the main horses are General Motors and Toyota with Ford pushed into third place.

Are these results preordained? Of course not. There are other laws of marketing that can also affect the results. Furthermore, your marketing programs can strongly influence your sales, provided they are in tune with the laws of marketing. When you're a weak No. 3, like Royal Crown, you aren't going to make much progress by going out and attacking the two strong leaders. They should have carved out a profitable niche for themselves. (Early on, for example, they could have focused on a diet cola.)

All this is obvious to successful marketers who concentrate on the top two rungs. Jack Welch, the legendary chairman and CEO of General Electric, said: "Only businesses that are No. 1 or No. 2 in their markets could win in the increasingly competitive global arena. Those that could not were fixed, closed, or sold." It's this kind of thinking that built companies like Procter & Gamble into the powerhouses they are. In 32 of its 44 product categories in the United States, Procter & Gamble commands the No. 1 or No. 2 brand.

Early on, in a developing market, the No. 3 or No. 4 positions look attractive. Sales are increasing. New, relatively unsophisticated customers are coming into the market. These customers don't always know which brands are the leaders, so they pick ones that look interesting or attractive. Quite often, these turn out to be the No. 3 or No. 4 brands.

As time goes on, however, these customers get educated. They want the leading brand, based on the naïve assumption that the leading brand must be better.

The customer believes that marketing is a battle of products. It's this kind of thinking that keeps the two brands on top: "They must be the best, they're the leaders."(This is bad news for a Chrysler comeback.)

But let's get back to Microsoft's big bet. Their first problem will be what to name their new horse. Yahoo? MSN? My advice would be to keep the Yahoo name and let the Microsoft brand remain the big horse in the software race.

Next up is a search for that obvious attacking strategy against Google. Now that will not be easy, but at least they are set up to be that strong No. 2 to No. 1.

Law of Resources

Without adequate funding, an obvious idea won't get off the ground.

If you have a powerful, obvious idea and you've picked up this book with the thought in mind that all you need is a little marketing help, this chapter will throw cold water on that thought.

Even the best idea in the world won't go very far without the money to get it off the ground. Inventors, entrepreneurs, and assorted idea generators seem to think that all their good ideas need is professional marketing help.

Nothing could be farther from the truth. Marketing is a game fought in the mind of the prospect. You need money to get into a mind. And you need money to stay in the mind once you get there.

You'll get farther with a mediocre idea and a million dollars than with a great idea alone.

Some entrepreneurs see advertising as the solution to the problem of getting into prospects' minds. Advertising is expensive. It cost $9,000 a minute to fight World War II. It cost $22,000 a minute to fight the Vietnam War. A one-minute commercial in the NFL Super Bowl will cost you $2.7 million.

Steve Jobs and Steve Wozniak had a great idea. But it was Mike Markkula's $91,000 that put Apple Computer on the map. (For his money, Markkula got one-third of Apple. He should have held out for half.)

Ideas without money are worthless. Well . . . not quite. But you have to use your idea to find the money, not the marketing help. The marketing can come later.

Some entrepreneurs see publicity as a cheap way of getting into prospects' minds. "Free advertising" is how they see it. Publicity isn't free. Rule of thumb: 5-10-20. A small public relations agency will want $5,000 a month to promote your product; a medium-sized agency, $10,000 a month; and a big-time agency, $20,000 a month.

Some entrepreneurs see venture capitalists as the solution to their money problems. But only a tiny percentage succeed in finding the funding they need this way.

Some entrepreneurs see corporate America as ready, willing, and financially able to get their offspring off the ground. Good luck, you'll need it. Very few outside ideas are ever accepted by large companies. Your only real hope is finding a smaller company and persuading it of the merits of your idea.

Remember: An idea without money is worthless. Be prepared to give away a lot for the funding.

In marketing, the rich often get richer because they have the resources to drive their ideas into the mind. Their problem is separating the good ideas from the bad ones, and avoiding spending money on too many products and too many programs.

Competition is fierce. The giant corporations put a lot of money behind their brands. Procter & Gamble and Philip Morris each spend more than $2 billion a year on advertising. General Motors spends $1.5 billion a year.

Life can be unfair for the smaller marketer facing larger competitors. Consider A&M Pet Products, a small company in Houston, Texas. A&M invented "clumping" cat litter, one of the most important breakthroughs in the category. The concept is simple. When cats use the litter box, this new type of litter clumps the waste into balls, which are easily scooped out and disposed of. There is no need to replace the entire box.

The brand, called Scoop Away, took off wherever it was introduced. This quickly got the attention of Golden Cat Corporation, which has the No. 1 cat litter brand, Tidy Cat.

Recognizing a threatening idea when they see one, Golden Cat introduced their own version of clumping cat litter, called Tidy Scoop. Not only did they jump on A&M's idea, they also borrowed the Scoop part of their brand name. (How unfair can you be?)

The winner of this cat fight will probably be determined by who has the most money to drive in the idea.

Unlike a consumer product, a technical or business product has to raise less marketing money because the prospect list is shorter and media is less expensive. But there is still a need for adequate funding for a technical product to pay for brochures, sales presentations, and trade shows as well as advertising.

Here is the bottom line: First get the idea, then go get the money to exploit it. Here are some shortcuts you could take:

- You can marry the money. Get your rich spouse to help fund your idea.
- You can divorce the money. Use your settlement to help fund your idea.
- You can find the money at home. Use your inheritance to fund your idea.
- You can share your idea by franchising it.

So far we've been talking about smaller companies and their fund-raising strategies. What about a rich company? How should it approach the Law of Resources? The answer is simple: Spend enough. In war, the military always errs on the high side. Do you know how many rations were left over after Operation Desert Storm? A lot. So it is in marketing. You can't save your way to success.

The more successful marketers frontload their investment. In other words, they take no profit for two or three years as they plow all earnings back into marketing.

Here's an obvious truth: Money makes the marketing world go round. If you want to be successful today, you'll have to find the money you need to spin those marketing wheels.

CHAPTER

9

Some Observations about Obvious Marketing Problems

This chapter outlines the obvious ideas that could be used to solve some highly publicized marketing problems. Some are observations. Several were searches for the obvious that I conducted.

Branding Lessons from General Motors: What Not to Do

Toyota is about to pass General Motors's seven-decade reign as the world's largest car producer by volume. That's right, 70 years of leadership is coming to an end. Today, Toyota has America's best-selling car—the Camry—and GM is struggling to make dwindling brands such as Buick and Pontiac mean something to consumers.

When something like this happens to a company of this stature, it's important to learn why it occurred. These are important lessons as, George Santayana warned: "Those who cannot remember the past are condemned to repeat it." I mentioned the GM brand schizophrenia problem in an earlier chapter. Here's a more detailed analysis of what went wrong.

When Alfred Sloan joined GM in 1924 as operating vice president, he inherited what he called an "irrational product line," one that had no guiding policy for the marketing of its many brands. The company's only objective was to sell cars. The brands stole volume from each other and, with the exception of Buick and Cadillac, all lost money.

Sloan immediately realized that GM had too many models and too much duplication and lacked a product policy. In one of the earliest examples of market segmentation, he reduced GM's offerings to five models, separated them by price grades, and emphasized individual brand image to entice customers into the GM family and move them up.

These distinct and strong brands allowed GM to capture more than 57 percent of the U.S. market by 1955. Aware that pursuing more market share could lead to antitrust actions and the threat of a breakup, GM fatefully shifted its strategy from making better cars to making more and more money from a relatively stable number of sales.

Nothing dramatized this new direction more than the concept of "badge engineering," or selling identical vehicles under different model names. This invention of GM's finance staff was a way to increase profits through uniformity, by, among other things, making parts interchangeable. Slowly but surely, the different brands lost the individual personalities that the company had so painstakingly established. At the same time, to improve their numbers (and bonuses), the GM divisions began to push the boundaries of the product policies that defined their brands: Chevrolet went up in price with fancier models, as did Pontiac. Buick and Oldsmobile offered cheaper versions. In time, GM was once again producing multiple cars of different brands that both looked and were priced alike. For GM, it was 1921 all over again.

Like BMW, Toyota pushed one brand in many forms. All these cars benefited by sharing one powerful differentiating idea: reliability. And when they went up into the super-premium category, it became a Lexus with all the Toyota identity carefully eliminated. Also, they have been quick to invest in new innovations such as the hybrid Prius and, the wheelchair friendly Porte, aimed at Japan's elderly population.

The bottom line in all this is that in the search for the obvious, *less is more.*

A successful brand has to stand for something. And the more variations you attach to it, the more you risk standing for nothing. This is especially true when what you add actually clashes with your perception. If Marlboro stands for cowboys out in Marlboro Country, how can they sell Marlboro Menthol or Marlboro Ultra Light cigarettes? Real cowboys don't smoke Menthols or Ultra Lights.

If Coke is the company that invented cola and is the owner of that special formula, how can they be the "Real Thing" when they offer a parade of new things including one called "Zero"? Why change that unique formula?

Should Wal-Mart try to sell more up-market products to compete with Target? No, that's not their market. (See the next section.)

Should Porsche risk its sports car image by selling SUVs? No, they are an iconic sports car brand.

Should Dell try to sell home electronics to compete with the Japanese and Koreans in this category? No, they sell computers directly to business.

Until companies come to grips with the simple fact that they don't really have an inordinate need to grow but an inordinate desire to grow (because of Wall Street), bad things will continue to happen. Slowly but surely, brands will lose their meaning as they try to become more.

What is happening to GM should be a lesson to all companies no matter how big and powerful they are. You cannot be everything to everybody and the more you try, the more you risk sinking the ship. History has proven this to be an obvious truth.

Can Wal-Mart Change?

Nothing has excited and riled up the advertising agency business as much as Wal-Mart's firing of a lady named Julie Roehm and the agency she hired.

It was all over the business press but nothing captured it better than the big headline in *Advertising Age* that proclaimed: "Unruly Julie and the scandal that rocked the ad world."

For those that missed the flap, Julie's problem was supposedly accepting fancy dinners in New York City, driving around in a fancy car with an agency head, pushing her favorite choice of agency, and even having an affair with her assistant. The agency world hasn't had excitement like this since the time that Mary Wells married the CEO of one of her big clients. (Mary always had a lot of style.)

Ms. Roehm was hired to help Wal-Mart change from a down-market, price-driven image to one that would attract the likes of those suburbanites shopping at Target and other slightly up-market establishments. Famous for her edgy, double-entendre marketing at Chrysler, she rode into the Wal-Mart culture like a tank driving through a brick wall.

Julie ascribed all her problems to being a change agent in an organization that didn't really want to change.

What was missing in all these articles was an analysis of whether Wal-Mart can or should change. I've written in the past that once a brand has established itself in the value or price category, it is almost impossible to go up-market and attract a group of customers that are already going for fancier brands. Wal-Mart is a mass merchandiser that clearly is all about "always low prices." (More on this in a later section.)

That's why people shop there.

And their culture, store layouts, and advertising push price for all it's worth. Retailers such as Ames or regional price players such as Caldor's tried to compete on price but are long deceased.

Target played it perfectly. Rather than go head-to-head with Godzilla, their obvious strategy was to offer "mass with class," or department store type merchandise for less. They used unique designs and nicer store layouts to attract those folks that were a bit more up-market and tended to look down on the Wal-Mart shopper. Remember, when you walk into a Wal-Mart, you are telling the world you are a price shopper. When you walk into a Target, you are telling the world you have a little more taste than a price buyer. When you walk into Neiman Marcus, you are telling the world that you have a lot of money and a great deal of taste.

Like everything else in this very competitive world, trying to be everything for everybody just doesn't work. You are what you are in the minds of your customers and prospects and leaving that position tends to generate confusion. Higher prices in a low-price store just suggest to your customers that you might be ripping them off.

The same goes for products. When Toyota went up-market with a $50,000 automobile, it gave it a different brand name

(Lexus) as did Honda (Acura). They didn't want their customers to feel they were buying puffed up Toyotas or Hondas.

So, someone at Wal-Mart recognized that change was not such a good thing for Wal-Mart to pursue. (Absolutely.) And with that realization, Julie and her new agency were no longer needed. In fact, if they hung around, all they would do is cause confusion among employees and customers. (Absolutely.)

Of course, this is past. What about the future? The answer to this question is now in the hands of Stephen Quinn, Wal-Mart's chief marketing officer. Already you're reading about suggestions being lobbed in by all the so-called experts. Be more targeted. Evolve. Stop making everything a commodity. My take is that if you're about value, talk more about value instead of price. You might even let your customers get a peek at what they do behind the shelves to offer that value. And you certainly can make the shopping experience better with friendlier service. (Think Southwest, which has flight attendants doing stand-up comedy.) What they shouldn't do is get fancy and try to go up-market against the likes of Target, especially as the country slides into a recession.

All this points to a simple truth: It's never too early or too late to correct a mistake. No matter what the embarrassment.

Confusion in Coke Land

Here's a very obvious problem.

Coca-Cola launched a rather strange campaign behind its Coca-Cola Zero product. It's based on the odd idea that the executives at Coca-Cola who sell Coca-Cola Classic want to hire lawyers to sue their coworkers who sell Coke Zero. To them it's "a clear case of taste infringement." In simple terms, the Classic marketing guys want to sue the Zero guys for producing a Coke with no calories that tastes as good as a Coke with calories.

But then you might say, "What about Diet Coke?" Good question. The grand strategy is to have a three-cola strategy—Classic, Diet, and Zero. This is not unlike Pepsi-Cola, which is pursuing the same idea. They have basic Pepsi, Diet Pepsi, Pepsi Max, and coming soon, Diet Pepsi Max.

What's going on here? In my estimation, nothing but confusion, and confusion is the enemy of effective marketing. This is the kind of stuff you often see when a category is flat or declining. All the marketing guys sit around, stare at complicated marketing research, and try and figure out ways to turn things around. Before you can say "segmentation," they are headed into endless line extensions designed to attract this segment or that customer group that the research has produced. Millions are spent in product development, marketing, and advertising and the business stays flat or even declines. Most of this activity revolves around existing customers who try these new offerings but eventually migrate back to their favorite version.

Think about it. If I drink Pepsi or Pepsi Max, why would I switch to Coke Zero? To get the taste of Coke Classic? It all makes little sense since I'm a Pepsi drinker. But, if I'm a Coke Classic drinker, I might be tempted to try a new cola with zero calories that tastes like the one I'm drinking. Who knows, but it all strikes me as just shuffling the deck chairs on a brand that's slowly sinking.

Even the Coke people admit to a bit of a cannibalization problem. They claim that 45 percent of Coke Zero drinkers are incremental rather than coming from Diet Coke drinkers. But what about Coke Classic drinkers? Any way you slice it, more than half of your drinkers were your original customers and now you are launching a campaign directly targeting

Coke Classic drinkers by dramatizing the fact that you can now get a Coke Classic taste with zero calories.

But they don't need to sit around and wait to see what happens. All they have to do is look over at the beer business and they have a pretty good view of their future. Budweiser and Miller have, over the years, produced endless line extensions trying to breathe some life into a declining category. They haven't generated any additional business. All they have done is cause confusion and muddied their brands. Budweiser once had a wonderful line, "This Bud's for you." The question became, which one do you have in mind? Now when you say, "The great taste of Coke," the question becomes, which one do you have in mind? Oh, forget it, I'll have a bottle of water.

The real victim of all this tinkering is the basic brand of Coca-Cola. As I wrote earlier, once upon a time they were "The Real Thing." This was a powerful differentiating idea that put Pepsi into the uncomfortable position of being a me-too brand. But, as you introduce more things such as a New Coke, a Diet Coke, a Vanilla or Cherry Coke, a Zero Coke, you can no longer be a real thing. You become a many things brand that stands for just being a cola. Obviously, Pepsi is also a cola so all you've done is level the playing field. Not good when you're the leader.

As I've written in *Differentiate or Die*, once you try to become everything, you become nothing in the mind. And without that differentiating idea, you'd better have a very low price. That's obvious.

Whither Newspapers?

The press in recent times has been all about the press. The Murdoch takeover of the *Wall Street Journal* has dominated the news. Is he a white knight or a spoiler? Beyond that, there have been many articles about the glum future of newspapers. Are they dying? Can the Internet save serious journalism?

The fact that these big newspapers have gone public makes things worse as Wall Street has weighed in with such things as attacks on the management of the *New York Times* and their lack of financial performance. Even Warren Buffett has pronounced that the present model—meaning print—isn't going to work. Being publicly owned puts all the focus on the numbers. And when you're trying to improve your numbers to make investors happy, you cut the things in which you should be investing such as people, promotion, and innovation.

No one has worked harder to improve the numbers than Donald Graham, the CEO of the *Washington Post*. He was one of the first to aggressively push into the digital world, yet critics say that Graham needs to move even faster to get the business online.

In an effort to recapture young readers, the *Post* in 2003 started a free weekday tabloid called the *Express*, which now publishes 185,000 copies a day. It's profitable. A year later the company acquired *El Tiempo Latino*, a Spanish-language weekly. It also publishes five paid-circulation suburban newspapers, 34 free suburban weeklies, 12 military newspapers, and real estate and auto guides. To squeeze a few more dollars out of its presses and trucks, the Post Co. distributes the *Wall Street Journal* in Washington, and it prints and circulates the local edition of the satirical newspaper the *Onion*. Bar mitzvah invitations may be next.

Yet, despite all this effort, print advertising revenue at the *Post* is six times that of Internet revenue. It's still about the paper. Needless to say, all this is one tough marketing problem.

Sometimes to solve a problem in one industry you have to study other analogous industries. In this case, I would look to the retail world. There are similarities. The store name is the brand where I go to shop. The newspaper name is the brand where I go to read. In both instances, I go for what's in each, so content is important. And in both instances, there are competitive forces that are causing great difficulties.

For example, good old Sears has been under enormous price pressure from the likes of Wal-Mart and Home Depot. Sears, through the years, built very powerful brands. Names like Die-Hard, Kenmore, Craftsman, and Weatherbeater paint are what make the difference for Sears. If they are to survive, their strategy should be to use these brands as "sold only at Sears." They can't compete on price or selection. (More on this in a later section.)

In my estimation, it's obvious that newspapers like the *New York Times* and the *Washington Post* have to pursue a similar "Read only at" strategy. They have to work hard at aggressively branding their writers such as the *New York Times*'s Tom Friedman, Maureen Dowd, or Paul Krugman. The more powerful these brands become, the more I'll have to buy the paper or pay to read them on the Internet. Also, the more I'll be able to charge for the paper. The sports world understands this. If Tiger Woods isn't in the tournament, television ratings take a big hit. Why do you think that Los Angeles team paid so much to get Beckham to kick a ball around?

Beyond the celebrity writers, newspapers have to talk more about their reporting staff: how many they have all around the world and their credentials. They have to point out that getting things accurate takes money, hard work, and lots of talent. (Stuff you can't get from the bloggers, cable television, or the *Daily Show*.) Many years ago, the *Wall Street Journal* ran an ad with the headline: "Every day the Kremlin gets 12 copies of the *Wall Street Journal*. Maybe they know something you don't know." Now that's the kind of advertising I would like to see more of on behalf of their hard-working staffs.

What newspapers have to realize is that in today's over-communicated world, it's as much about content as about news. It's as much about celebrity as it is about unknown reporters. It's as much about how you get the news as it is about just printing it. This might be a tough reality to face for the owners of these papers but the barbarians are at the gates. You've got to wheel out and aggressively promote your big guns, your organization, and why you should be read.

And, if you keep your readers, the advertisers will come.

Celebrities Who "Un-Sell" Products

Celebrity reporters are a reason to read a newspaper. But a celebrity name alone isn't much of a reason to buy anything.

Consider a recent Macy's program that launched a major celebrity effort to try and restore some luster to its somewhat unsuccessful effort to build a national chain of 825 stores under the Macy's brand. They developed advertising that featured celebrities such as Martha Stewart, Sean Combs, Jessica Simpson, Donald Trump, and Emeril Lagasse. All have something in common: They sell name-branded items at Macy's.

Will this do the trick? Will this jazz up the department store category under attack from the mass merchandisers or the specialty retailers? My feeling is that the answer to this question is, "Not likely." Here are the reasons.

First of all, successful celebrity brands have to have a very direct connection to the celebrity. It has to make sense to the prospect. Michael Jordan selling Nike sneakers is the Mount Everest of marketing.

Why has the Air Jordan brand seen such success year in and year out? Michael could play basketball and jump like few others could. And sneakers are critical to that skill. The prospect figured that those sneakers helped Michael do what he could do and some of that magic might be in those expensive basketball shoes. Shaquille O'Neal has a sneaker brand that has made very little impact for the simple reason that he doesn't jump very high or move that well. No connection. On the other hand, his efforts to sell a pain reliever probably worked out quite well. Everyone realizes that there's a lot of pain in that big body game.

Consider Tiger Woods and his Nike golf balls. When his name wasn't connected to Nike golf products, their golf balls didn't sell. As soon as the world saw what balls he was using, they suddenly became a lot more popular. (Though not as popular as the category leader, Titleist, that has the most professional golfers using them.) But can Tiger Woods sell Buicks? No way, for the simple reason that the prospect sees no natural connection. He was just paid to be in the commercial and everyone knows that with his money he should be driving a Bentley, not a Buick.

That said, let's get back to Macy's. Is there a natural connection to Martha Stewart's home products? Sure. As a result, they might sell some of these items. But they won't sell anywhere as many as the known brands of cookware and china sell. Donald Trump has a natural connection to real estate, not suits. Besides, not only does he always look like he's in the same clothes, most people spend all their time looking at his hair, not what he's wearing. And, with his money, he's probably wearing custom tailored suits. Jessica Simpson shoes? No big deal. Emeril Lagasse cookware? Sure, but now you're competing with Martha's cookware.

The bottom line is that all these celebrity brands aren't enough to make Macy's a cool place to visit. And then there's the question of what about all the other stuff on sale at the store. Will I pick up a celebrity item and walk past all those other counters? I have a clear perception of why I should go to Wal-Mart (low prices) or Target (department store products for less) or Nordstrom (service) or Saks (prestige products). Macy's is in dire need of a clear positioning or differentiation strategy and those celebrities aren't it. If they and other celebrities all shopped there, maybe. But the fact that they sell their stuff there isn't much of a reason to pass up all those other stores.

Finally, there is the issue that sometimes celebrities can "un-sell" products and cause problems for their sponsor.

James Garner was selling beef until he had a widely publicized heart attack and the resulting triple bypass. Uh, oh!

Reebok spent $25 million on an ad campaign for two track and field stars—Dan O'Brien and Dave Johnson. At the Olympics, Dan failed to capture a single medal, Dave only a bronze. Uh, oh!

Tennis star Martina Hingis was an endorser for an Italian sneaker and tennis gear company until she sued them, claiming the shoes were the cause of her injuries. Uh, oh!

Kobe Bryant was in McDonald's Sprite and Nutella promotion until he was charged with sexual assault. Uh, oh!

Michael Vick was one of those Nike athletes until he was convicted of dog fighting. Uh, oh!

Unfortunately, there's always the danger that your celebrity will do something that will embarrass your branding program. You can fire them but damage can still be done. (Nike quickly took away Michael Vick's "Swoosh.")

One of my favorite celebrity programs is that of Betty Crocker. She's been selling baked goods for decades. And because she's make-believe, she never goes astray and never wants a raise. And the last time I checked with General Mills, she still gets mail from her fans.

That Bewildering Beer Business

For years I've been writing about the problems of line exten-sion. Let's review the bidding.

In *Positioning: The Battle for Your Mind*, there are two chap-ters on the problems of line extension.

In *The 22 Immutable Laws of Marketing*, it became the single most violated law.

In *The New Positioning*, I wrote about the problem as a "matter of perspective." I pointed out that the difference in views on this subject is how a product is perceived inside and outside of a company. Companies look at their brands from an economic point of view. To gain cost efficiencies and trade acceptance, they are quite willing to turn a highly focused brand, one that stands for a certain type of product or idea, into an unfocused brand that represents two or three or more types of products or ideas. We look at the issue of line exten-sion from the point of view of the mind. The more variations you attach to the brand, the more the mind loses focus. Grad-ually, a brand like Chevrolet comes to mean nothing at all. The simple bottom line: A brand that's many things can't be one thing.

No one category has ignored all this as has the beer busi-ness. Consider Miller beer. What started out in 1978 as a clas-sic pilsner has become a portfolio of beers. Each brand in the portfolio suffers from a bad case of line extension. If you want a Miller beer, the next question will be "Which one?" At what point do you want Miller Lite, Miller Lite Ice, Miller Genuine Draft, Miller Genuine Draft Lite, Miller High Life, Miller High Life Lite, or Miller High Life Ice?

Oh, forget it, I'll have a Budweiser.

They also own the Jacob Leinenkugel Brewing Company. The last time I checked, it has the same problem—you have to figure out whether you want a Leinenkugel's Original Premium, Leinenkugel's Light, Leinenkugel's Northwoods Lager, Leinenkugel's Genuine Bock (seasonal), Leinenkugel's Red Lager, Leinenkugel's Honey Weiss, Leinenkugel's Berry Weiss (seasonal), Leinenkugel's Hefeweizen (draft only), or Leinenkugel's Creamy Dark.

Oh, forget it, I'll have a Corona.

You might say, "Why should the beer people listen to you?" Good point. But even support from the *Harvard Business Review* failed to slow down the line extension express. And their verdict was severe: "Unchecked product-line expansion can weaken a brand's image, disturb trade relations, and disguise cost increases." And nowhere has this damage been as visible as in the beer business. Miller has all but destroyed what Miller means. Budweiser has too many "Buds for you," and Bud Light is eating into basic Budweiser. And what in the world is Bud Select? Coors Light has pretty much done in Regular Coors.

And they wonder why the beer business has been flat all these years. With so much confusion, it has become, "Oh, forget it, I'll have a bottle of water."

But now comes the ultimate irony. For years, makers of small-batch "craft" beers have been chipping away at the market share of the three beer giants. Now the big brewers are playing the same game. But this time, they avoid using the parent company's name on the labels for their craft beers. Anheuser-Busch, for example, lists Green Valley Brewing Co. as the maker of Wild Hop Lager. Jacob Leinenkugel Brewing Co. is owned by SABMiller PLC. Blue Moon Brewing Co. is a subsidiary of Molson Coors Brewing Co.

And without their big brand names, the retail sales of these big company craft beers grew nearly three times the rate of the real craft beers.

Does that mean that the big brewers have at long last seen the errors in their line extension ways?

Don't bet on it.

Whither Starbucks?

It looks like things are tightening up in Latte Land. The economy and competition are making Starbucks' glorious run a lot more difficult.

The first sign of trouble came from the stock market. Starbucks' share price has been cut in half in the past year after more than a decade of nearly continuous growth.

The next sign was the firing of their CEO, who is to be replaced by the man who built the business from just four stores, Howard Schultz. Now they have 15,000 stores in 43 countries. What Mr. Schultz is learning is that the bigger you are, the harder it is to manage. He promoted rapid growth and he now has to clean up the problems he probably fostered by opening far too many stores.

On the competitive front, Dunkin' Donuts and now McDonald's are threatening to take more and more business by offering a good cup of coffee at considerably less than what you pay at Starbucks.

I found it interesting that Mr. Schultz is not too concerned about competition. He feels that the problem is with Starbucks itself and all he needs is to fix it. In many ways, he is right but I'm not sure that he is focused on the right problem.

As I see it, when you are selling a very expensive product as compared to the competition, you are always faced with having to supply your customer with a rationale about why it is worth the extra money. When someone buys a $60,000 Mercedes to impress their friends and neighbors, you have to rationalize this purchase by telling your prospect that this car has amazing engineering that is worth the money. If you are selling a $10,000 Rolex watch, you have to supply the rationale that each Rolex takes a year to build. No one wants to feel they are being ripped off.

Starbucks never had real competition so they felt no pressure to tell people why their coffee costs so much. They figured if they open more stores people will come. Well, recent sales indicate that people are beginning not to come, probably because of the economy. In fact, they were so successful they didn't even feel the need to advertise and have only started to do this recently. Unfortunately, their ads haven't said very much about their coffee. And if McDonald's does a reasonable job with their latte, the question of "Why pay so much?" could become a big issue. I'm not saying that a Starbucks customer would be happy in a Dunkin' Donuts or, heaven forbid, a McDonald's. But, if they come up with even an almost-as-good product, questions will be asked about the value of those expensive cups of coffee.

Ironically, Howard Schultz wrote a memo to the CEO in 2007 titled "The Commoditization of the Starbucks Experience." While it was about "watering down of the Starbucks experience," I feel that he had the right word in "commoditization." If the market doesn't begin to hear from Starbucks about why their coffee is worth the money, the market will begin to think that coffees and lattes are becoming commoditized. McDonald's has a fancy machine similar to Starbucks' machine. So why should they pay so much more for the coffee from a Starbucks machine? Aren't all the machines producing similar coffee? Is it just a matter of machines? Hey, for that matter, I can now buy an expensive coffee machine and do it myself.

You see the problem. Starbucks has been so busy building stores that it failed to build perception about why their coffee is better and worth the money. I suspect there is a story there but they have failed to tell it with drama. There's an old axiom in marketing, "What you advertise, what you sell, and what you make your money on can be three different things." I go to Starbucks for the coffee, not CDs or movies or even food. That's why their coffee is what they should advertise.

What Howard Schultz has to do is obvious. By not telling their coffee story, they have a potential commoditization problem. Now he has to fix it by telling that story.

Marketing with Other People's Money

One of the siren songs of marketing is the opportunity to earn some extra money by licensing your brand name. Someone comes up to you and offers you a deal you can't refuse. After all, you're playing with other people's money. It's also long-term trouble for your brand.

It all begins, in many instances, with a licensing agency that goes out and hustles your brand. Here's an actual example from a web site:

> We are the licensing agency for Pratt & Whitney Corporation. Pratt is interested in licensing companies the rights to produce and market products under the Pratt & Whitney brand name. Categories that we are currently in discussions with companies about include power generators, aviation tools (power, air, hand tools), pilot accessories, welders, air compressors, power washers, tow units, engine stands, aviation electronics (headsets, gps, radios, etc.), outdoor power equipment and small engines. If you are interested in becoming a Pratt & Whitney licensee to capitalize on the worldwide recognition of the Pratt & Whitney brand, then please contact me.

There you go. Instead of focusing on being the No. 2 jet engine in the world and figuring out how to sell against GE jet engines, they want to become everything they can think of and then some.

Not good marketing but it's someone else's money.

"Fashion's big guns will put their name on just about anything," writes Susan Chandler in a U.K. article on brands.

"Designers aren't content to merely dress their customers any more. They want to furnish their clients' homes, outfit their children, and formulate the shade of lipstick they wear. American designer Ralph Lauren was a pioneer in the 'lifestyle brand' trend in the 1980s, but nearly every A-list designer today, from Giorgio Armani to Stella McCartney, has their name on sunglasses, jewelry, handbags, and perfume.

"Those who do it well make a lot of money. But creating line extensions is a risky strategy that can dilute a brand's power if it is overdone. Calvin Klein and Bill Blass discovered that years ago when they signed a bunch of licensing agreements that allowed manufacturers to slap their names on inexpensive goods. Their cachet eroded."

Pierre Cardin has lent his name to just about everything—at the expense, say some, of much of his credibility. He is known all over the world due to his penchant for stamping his name on everything from golf clubs and frying pans to binoculars and orthopedic mattresses. While most designers content themselves with fragrance, accessories, and underwear, Cardin has amassed more than 800 licensees around the globe, and earns royalties on Pierre Cardin luggage, ceramics, and cooker hoods. And when he acquired the famous Maxim's restaurant in Paris in 1981, he made merry with that name, too, applying his creative talents to such Maxim products as flowers and sardines. (Yes, Pierre Cardin sardines.) One product you won't find around anymore is Pierre Cardin wine.

People who tried it said, "It tasted all right but it had a per-fumy smell."

Not good marketing but it's someone else's money.

Donald Trump is the current king of silly licensing. He made his name negotiating gold-plated real estate deals, but when it comes to selling other goods, the tycoon doesn't always have the Midas touch. A line of golf clothing sold in Macy's was discontinued. And a man's fragrance unveiled in 2004 with fanfare and also sold at Macy's is no longer in pro-duction. (Who wants to smell like Donald Trump?) Marty Brochstein, editor of the *Licensing Letter*, put it very well when he said, "If I'm a golfer, whose clothes do I want to buy, Tiger Woods or Donald Trump?"

Tracking the performance of Trump merchandise is not always easy because sales figures are not made public. Ironi-cally, the one area where you can measure performance is the Trump Casinos. They have been heading south for some time while losing a lot of money for a lot of folks.

Not good marketing but it's someone else's money.

Richard Branson is sort of a Donald Trump on steroids when it comes to licensing the Virgin brand. He has 50,000 people working on Virgin brands all over the world in all types of business. (One, Virgin Cola, is no longer with us.) But as the Brits would say, "Sir Richard is in a spot of bother." In Branson's home base, the United Kingdom, his Virgin empire is being battered from all sides, from its squabbles with Rupert Murdoch over satellite TV to loss of a cross-country rail fran-chise. Despite an advertising campaign fronted by the Holly-wood actress Uma Thurman, Virgin Media, created out of the former NTL cable company, is losing customers and is also subject to a takeover approach from private equity company Carlyle Group that could see the Virgin name ditched. (The stock is also headed south.)

Meanwhile in America and Asia, Sir Richard is launching Virgin brands of discount airline service. For his name, he takes a 20 percent ownership stake and his partners put up the capital. All I can say is good luck in those discount airline jungles.

But the beat goes on with other people's money.

Toy company Hasbro Inc. has struck a deal to license its Playskool brand to baby care products including disposable wipes and diapers, and CVS drugstores will begin selling these Playskool products this fall at more than 6,100 national stores. A toy diaper? My guess is that these baby-care products won't do very well against the likes of Pampers and Huggies.

Will it ever end? I doubt it. As my father once advised me, "There's a sucker born every day and two to sell him."

You Can't Go Up-Market

A few new items caught my eye recently.

Zale's, king of middle market jewelry, tried to go up-market and sell more expensive jewelry. They had little success.

Wrangler, a brand that sells $15 jeans in Wal-Mart tried to sell $190 jeans at Barney's. They had little success.

And speaking of Wal-Mart, they recently launched a marketing effort to sell higher priced merchandise as a way to get business from Target. They will have little success.

What these companies fail to understand is that it is exceptionally difficult to take a well-established brand up in price or value. The automobile people have a long history of failure in this regard.

As previously mentioned, years ago Cadillac tried to take a $50,000 Allante up against Mercedes. They had little success.

Also mentioned, Volkswagen tried to take a $60,000 Phaeton up against Mercedes and BMW. They had no success.

They already own the Audi brand so why try and compete with them? What all these companies fail to understand is that it is not what you want to do, it is what your customers will let you do. But, even more importantly, it's what their perceptions will let you do.

As I wrote earlier, Wal-Mart's perceptions are all about low price, which is the opposite of higher quality. Target offers "mass with class." People perceive them as offering department store, well-designed products for less. They will never trust fancier Wal-Mart products that cost more.

As I've already mentioned, the classic success story about going up-market was that of Toyota when they wanted to introduce a super-premium car. Unlike Cadillac and Volkswagen, they avoided the perception trap. The new car was called a Lexus; they set up a new breed of fancy dealerships and said at the outset that a Lexus dealer could not be closer than 10 miles to a Toyota dealer. Today, the Lexus brand is the leading super-premium car in America. I suspect that a few people don't know that it is made by Toyota. But most see these two brands as totally separate operations. Now that's success.

Let me explain it another way. To cope with the product explosion, people have learned to mentally rank products and brands. Perhaps this can best be visualized by imagining a series of ladders. On each step is a brand name. And each different ladder represents a different product category.

Some ladders have many steps. (Seven is the maximum.) Others have few, if any, because there is low interest in the category. (Caskets are an example of a no-rung ladder category.)

A competitor who wants to increase its share of the business must either dislodge the brand on the rung above (a task that is usually impossible) or somehow relate its brand to the other company's position.

Yet, too many companies embark on marketing and advertising programs as if the competitor's position did not exist. They advertise their products in a vacuum and are disappointed when their messages fail to get through.

Mentally moving up the ladder can be extremely difficult if the brands above have a strong foothold and no leverage or positioning strategy is applied.

An advertiser who wants to introduce a new product category must carry in a new ladder.

What you cannot do is try and put your brand name on two different ladders at the same time. People just can't keep things sorted out that way. So your only hope is to leave your existing brand on its mental ladder and take a new brand over to that up-market ladder in your category.

What's at play here is that once people establish those ladders, they are loath to change their minds or rearrange them. They say that, "I know what you are and I have you stored in the right place. Don't confuse the issue."

There's also a flipside to all this because you *can* come down in price and value with a brand. Many years ago, Cadillac was successfully challenged by a car called a Packard. Then, Packard decided to sell a cheaper Packard. It was a wild success for one year. But that was the game because they never were able to sell expensive Packards again. There was no more "prestige" attached to the car so the choice became Cadillac at the top of the market. You can go down but you can't go up again.

But nothing dramatizes this "you can't go up" principle like the current efforts of Korea's carmaker Hyundai and its Kia subsidiary. They have been through four management shakeups in three years in their American operation. The problem is Korean management that wants to move up into the low end of the luxury business and sell cars over $25,000. U.S. executives have told their counterparts in Seoul that the two brands are not strong enough to move up and sell into that price range. These warnings have been ignored. Prediction: Little sales success and more management churning in the future.

Conglomerate Schizophrenia

An interesting article in the *Wall Street Journal* reported on what they called "The Conglomerates Conundrum." This was about ads aimed at investors that required "putting a face on the faceless."

How does a Tyco or a United Technologies or even a General Electric get investors excited about a company in multiple businesses? The answer: with great difficulty. A better analysis of the inherent problem in these kinds of programs is that you try to advertise a client with multiple personalities. And it's exceptionally difficult for an analyst to get his or her head around these types of schizophrenic companies. How do I evaluate all these different businesses and assign a buy or hold or even a sell recommendation? How does an investor do the same? You might like one personality but dislike the other personalities. It's all very confusing.

This has been an age-old problem that has led corporate America to act like an accordion. First, they expand and acquire a lot of diverse businesses. Diversification is good but then they realize not only is it hard to manage all these different businesses and competitors but Wall Street doesn't understand them. Next, they contract and sell off all their acquisitions. Focus is good. Wall Street gets it—at least for a while.

The standard reason for all these sell-the-stock activities is "We have to create a brand for the parent company." Another favorite is exposing a need to "educate the public investors and analysts about our far-reaching operations." Well, history has pretty much proven that these types of multimillion-dollar programs rarely live up to expectations.

The real reason for many of these programs is what I call "the cocktail party problem." Consider the following: A CEO of a large corporation is meeting and greeting people at some fancy event. Someone asks him or her, what company are you with? When you announce the name of the company and all you get is a blank stare or a "What do you sell?" question, the CEO gets uncomfortable. If that tableau is repeated a number of times, trust me, pretty soon the company will begin to plan a "we have got to tell our story" program.

I hate to be a killjoy, but I think most of these programs are a waste of money. A company is in business to generate customers for its products and services, not to sell stock. If you do the former very well, chances are the latter will take care of itself.

Consider one of my favorite companies, United Technologies. This is a company with some of the best brands in the business world—Carrier Air Conditioning, Otis Elevator, Pratt & Whitney jet engines, Sikorsky helicopters. Business is good and their stock is considerably above, say, General Electric, but it's not high enough to make them happy. So they are launching a $20 million corporate campaign with the tag line, "You can see everything from here." I'm not so sure what that means but anyone who's buying any of their brands could care less about the parent company. In fact, it's the opposite. What they have is a powerful portfolio of specialists. Carrier, Sikorsky, and Otis practically invented the categories of air conditioning, helicopters, and elevators. People are impressed with them because they see them as specialists, not a part of a big conglomerate. And you don't want to undermine those perceptions because people perceive specialists as the best because that's all they do.

That's exactly GE's problem. They have a bunch of businesses that all have the same name. This puts them in the generalist category and generalists tend to lose to specialists in the market. (The small appliance specialists drove GE out of the business.)

But don't think I'm against all corporate advertising. What United Technologies could do is run a program in a magazine like *Forbes* about "the power of specialists." And why they nurture them and stay out of their way. That kind of program would differentiate them from all those other conglomerates. And if people are impressed with that business strategy, United Technologies might even see their stock go up. Because what they are doing is exactly what should be done to run a multiple business company.

Can Sears Be Saved?

The fabled retail brand of Sears is in trouble. Now owned by hedge fund executive Edward Lampert, they announced their latest turnaround, which included the departure of their CEO. Lampert's plan is to reorganize the 121-year-old retailer into business units with "broad authority to shape their own future." I'm not sure what that means but to me it looks like big trouble if their big brands such as Kenmore and Craftsman can cut deals with other retailers. It could spell the end of the Sears brand as we've known it for all these years. To me, Sears has never pursued the only obvious strategy available to them. Somewhere along the line they forgot what made Sears famous.

No, it wasn't the catalogue. That was the correct answer several generations ago. In modern times, Sears was one of the few retailers, if not the only retailer, that built real brands. People went to Sears to buy Kenmore appliances, Craftsman tools, DieHard batteries, Weatherbeater paint, and Roadhandler tires.

Once there, they bought other stuff like Levi's or Sony TVs. But it was those brands, sold only at Sears, that made the difference.

But in recent years, there hasn't been much in the way of brand building coming out of Sears. Quite the contrary— "Brand Central" talked about offering everybody's brands (wrong strategy). And the "Soft Side" featured no brands (wrong strategy).

It would appear that Sears has not learned one of marketing's basic lessons. *Never forget what made you famous.*

Because there has been a hiatus in brand building at Sears, it seems obvious that what's needed is to revisit each brand and figure out how to revitalize and strengthen it. As I indicated earlier, they should take advantage of Kenmore's leadership and position it as the No. 1 family of appliances in the end. They should do the same for Craftsman, which is America's favorite brand of tools by far. Perhaps it's time for a next generation of DieHard battery that dies a little harder? Maybe their Weatherbeater paints could use some sprucing up?

If they do a good job with their brands, more people will go to Sears. And if designers improve the store's layout, people might spend more time buying other things.

And while they're at it, maybe they should invest in a new brand or two? Interestingly, they sort of did that when they bought the Lands' End clothing line although being a catalog brand does cause some confusion. They certainly could launch a specialty truck tire in their automotive department. What I wouldn't do is spend a lot of money on the Sears brand. That's only where you go to find those "sold only at Sears" brands. If you allow these brands to be sold elsewhere, you have no differentiating strategy for Sears.

With that kind of a back-to-the-future strategy, their obvious position for the store would be: *Home of America's favorite brands.*

One other problem that Mr. Lampert faces is, what to do with Kmart? That also calls for an obvious solution: abandon its Kmart brand and convert the stores to Sears. With the likes of Wal-Mart, Target, and J.C. Penney's as competitors, Kmart's future will never be bright. Maybe Martha Stewart's brand would do better in a revamped Sears store than in a struggling Kmart.

Turning around one troubled brand is tough. Turning around two in the same category is impossible.

Extreme Makeover: America's Image

In today's hypercompetitive world, countries are becoming important brands in terms of tourism and business and it doesn't take too many trips out in the world to sense that Brand America is in trouble. If you're interested in the numbers, the Pew Research people have them all. The basic message: America's image is in a dramatic decline just about everywhere. This is not a good thing in a world being driven by the global economy. Whether you're selling airplanes, computers, power plants, or automobiles, it's not helpful when people dislike the country of origin. It gives your global competitors an emotional edge.

No one appreciates this more than Brand America's salesforce, namely the U.S. State Department.

Some years ago, I was asked by them to develop a marketing program to help diplomatic officers better sell America, its products, and its efforts to the world community. It is something that is desperately needed. The obvious problem was that the only concept attached to the United States is: "The world's last superpower." All this expression does is portray us as the world's bully. And some of the administration's language and policies only reinforced this perception. In China, for example, the media often refers to America as the global police.

Coming up with a better marketing concept was fairly simple. Go to the world community with a program that offered more benefits, not threats. The obvious strategy was to have President Bush say to the world that we are shifting from self-vision to a new world vision simply expressed as: "Helping the world to be a safer, freer, and more prosperous place." That's what everyone wants and we can help deliver those benefits. Here's a simple but wise observation as to why this approach should work. It's from the *New York Times* columnist Thomas Friedman, who wrote, "If you convey to people that you really want them to succeed, they will take any criticism you dish out. If you convey that you really hold them in contempt, you can tell them that the sun is shining and they won't listen to you."

I even showed the diplomatic officers how they could use this strategy to help sell policies. The road map to peace in the Palestine/Israeli conflict was about security. Reconstructing Afghanistan was about prosperity as was supporting Turkey for membership in the European Union. Supporting women's rights in the Middle East and the youth in Iran was about freedom. Every basic policy worth pursuing could be supported by this overall concept.

Interestingly, many programs in the State Department were already heading in this direction. In terms of safety, for example, America's public diplomacy brought in conflict resolution experts to work with and train people in techniques to prevent violence in South Africa. In terms of prosperity, a faulty legal system scares off investors. Public diplomacy assisted Chile in promoting judicial reform and a transparent legal system. They have become one of South America's most prosperous economies.

There are some that might argue with this idea. Why is the world our problem? Why make the world better? The reasons are obvious. From a business point of view, a more orderly world will decrease our enormous expenses in security and defense. It will expand our income via trade and thus increase our employment. In other words, it's good for business and it's good for America.

Unfortunately, as I warned the State Department, you need the right people in the room to sell a strategy. As you saw in an earlier chapter, the CEO has to be involved. But, at that time, America's top management was preoccupied with invading Iraq, not improving America's image.

To follow the law of resources, they also had to increase our efforts and investments in public diplomacy. We've let this function dramatically slide in recent years. A former Russian Foreign Minister made an important observation, "America is like a big business that decided it doesn't need a PR department. Every business needs PR. Even a monopoly needs PR."

My only concern is whether they will be selling the right thing. "Democracy," as nice as it sounds to us, is not what everyone wants. (For example, try selling that idea in China.) What people do want are the benefits of a good democracy: security, freedom, and prosperity. And of the three, my bet is that prosperity would be the most popular. That would be a good choice as, in my estimation, it is the ultimate weapon in the war on terrorism. Terrorist activities are bad for business.

"Un-Marketing" Drugs

Reducing drug usage in America has been the longest running, most unsuccessful marketing program in history. I wrote earlier about "repositioning the competition." Well, let's apply that strategy in the so-called "drug war" in an attempt to suggest a better approach.

Millions of Americans want to consume drugs and we've repeatedly pointed out the difficulty of trying to change people's minds.

How do you "reduce the demand" for drugs? The obvious strategy is to find a way to hang a very negative idea on drug use. That means a repositioning strategy is necessary.

Put on your marketing hat. You've just received a call from a new president. You're to head up a new government-sponsored communications program to replace the hodgepodge of a program that has had little impact on reducing demand.

Obviously, some changes are called for if progress is to be made. And progress is desperately needed. After years of effort and billions of dollars spent in law enforcement, it would appear there is only one long-term way to decrease the usage and sale of drugs in America: You have to find a way to decrease demand.

Decreasing supply only increases the price and the profit potential for suppliers willing to take the risks. Since the product cost is so low and the return so high, experience shows that there is no effective way, outside of legalizing drugs, that will force illegal drug suppliers out of business. For every drug dealer you shut down, two will open up. So the question is, "What's the strategy?"

Let's start with a quick monitoring of the trends in substance abuse. As in any problem, you don't always just focus on the product at hand. You try to get a feeling for the entire category. We call this the *context* of the market.

In this case, the smoking of cigarettes offers important parallels in looking for the answer to the problem of drug consumption. Like drugs, cigarettes introduce a foreign substance into the body. They can be addictive, and it is widely accepted that they are bad for you. In fact, they have been reported to kill 50 times as many Americans as drugs do.

The main differences between cigarettes and drugs are that cigarettes are legal as well as an important revenue source for the government. As a result, just about everyone knows that cigarettes are bad for you, yet cigarette sales, while declining, have not shown a steep decline. (Today, cigarettes kill only 45 times as many Americans as drugs do.)

It would appear that the educational approach that presents the health hazards of smoking has failed to overcome the image enhancement that cigarette companies have promised in their advertising. Eliminating cigarettes from broadcast advertising has hurt the industry's ability to launch new brands, but the message still gets through via a wide array of media still available to cigarette advertisers.

On the basis of the cigarette lesson, you can probably surmise that an educational "bad for you" approach might not be a good tactic to dramatically reduce demand if drugs continue to be perceived as "in." The same can be said for the advertising industry's $500 million effort that for the most part also says "bad for you" in a number of different ways.

What this monitoring of the cigarette experience shows you is that the traditional "top-down" approach of telling people what's bad for them rarely works. In other words, it's time to shift the battlefield.

What appears to be more of an influence on consumption of a product is its social message. (Before World War II, every star in a Hollywood movie smoked. Today, few smoke on film.)

This insight offers an opportunity. Unlike cigarette manufacturers, drug producers and sellers cannot use advertising to promote a fashionable image for their drugs. On the other hand, government can use advertising to make drugs less and less fashionable to use.

If America runs true to form, this will dramatically reduce demand. When a product is "out" in America, it doesn't sell. Now to your important decision: What concept can you use to begin to make drugs unfashionable?

When you study the situation, one obvious idea jumps out as a repositioning strategy to employ. It has been widely demonstrated that drug use is a one-way street. Heavy users are in danger of losing their jobs, losing their friends, losing their families, losing their self-esteem, losing their freedom, and eventually losing their lives.

What this sets up is a simple play on words that can be a two-edged sword against the drug dealers. One that points out the bad things that drugs can do to you while presenting them in the context of a social image.

The obvious idea: *Drugs are for losers.*

If the perception that drugs are for losers can be established, a mortal blow at demand will be struck. If America disdains anything, it's a loser. Underdogs are acceptable, but winners are what America admires most and what everyone aspires to.

Now it's time for you to turn your repositioning idea into a national strategy by figuring out who should deliver this message to America. The natural choice is to have ex-drug users or relatives of users tell their sad and moving stories. The natural medium is television with its emotional and personal impact.

Celebrities and sports stars who have had publicized drug problems could be asked to participate in this program. For example, ex-baseball-star Denny McLain talking about how he went to jail and lost his freedom, John Belushi's wife talking about how her husband lost his life or a family member discussing the death of River phoenix.

At the end of every commercial, the speaker would look in the camera and say, "Drugs are for losers." As more and more famous and infamous people deliver that message, America will begin to see that drugs take you down, not up.

When this happens, the demand for drugs will start to go down and the drug business will become a lot less profitable. This is bound to make organized crime think twice about the risk/return ratio in the drug business.

Brand China at the Crossroads

In a recent visit to China, I had a sense that China's high-speed manufacturing machine was in need of an obvious course change to avoid a very rough road ahead.

Built as a low-cost machine aimed at the OEM market, China is truly the world's workshop. But the explosive growth has come at a high price. There are big environmental problems of factory pollution and energy shortages. There are quality control problems that are causing many customers to rethink China as a reliable supplier. There are "social responsibility" issues that have led the government to force entrepreneurs to pay higher wages. Managed growth and more controls are in the offing.

But here's the difficulty: All these problems will only increase China's manufacturing costs. That in turn will force manufacturers in China to shift production to lower cost areas in the country or move to places such as Vietnam. Because there is always someone out there who will do it for less, if you live by low cost alone, you will die by low cost.

China must consider taking what can be called the "Branding Highway." This takes them to where they can start to build local and international brands that offer more than just low price. In other words, instead of making products for someone else, they make them for themselves. But this road also leads them into the land of intense competition.

Internationally, they will be competing with companies that have been competing for years in markets all around the world. If they make a mistake, these companies will run right over them. Locally, they will be competing against many competitors that are only too willing to cut their price.

Consider the current China price war over automobiles. There are 19 brands that have less than 1 percent market share. This is a recipe for no profits.

Peter Drucker, the father of management consulting, once advised that only two business functions produce new customers: marketing and innovation. All other functions are expenses. This means Chinese companies have to learn about marketing. They will have to learn about *positioning* or how to win battles in the mind of a customer and prospect. They will have to learn about *marketing warfare* or how to cope with competition. They will have to learn about *differentiation* or how to figure out what makes you different from your competitors. But most of all, they have to understand that it's not just about low price but about added value or creating that reason as to why a product is worth a little more than competitive products.

Consider Tsingtao beer, a 104-year-old Chinese brand that faces more and more international brand competition. What makes them different is the fact that the Germans built the original brewery. Obviously, they are the "Chinese German Beer," which makes them very different and very good. After all, all the world knows that German beer is the best. To compete, Tsingtao must make sure everyone knows about their German heritage.

Many of those differentiating reasons are found in research and development, which brings me to *innovation*. In America,

Silicon Valley is the hotbed of innovation or new ideas. In India, you'll find this kind of activity in Bangalore. Where is China's Silicon Valley? Innovation is all about a lot of smart people thinking of exciting new ideas. And these kinds of people like to work in an area that has other smart people thinking up new ideas. But all of this activity costs money. And if you sell your products as cheaply as possible, you will have little left to invest in research and development much less the cost of marketing that's needed to sell your new innovations.

Consider Mindray Medical International, a Chinese medical equipment manufacturer. They have set aside a good chunk of their profits for research and development. They now export ultrasound imaging and blood test equipment to 140 countries. That's the road to success.

Some Chinese companies are buying established non-Chinese brands from different places around the world. This may be a good strategy but what's often available are not the winners but the also-ran brands that someone wants to unload. So they are faced with the task of how to turn a loser into a winner. This is no easy accomplishment for people unskilled in marketing.

Consider Lenovo that bought the IBM PC brand and renamed it. They now face HP, Dell, Apple, and ACER (which bought the Gateway brand). It will take a lot of innovation and marketing to succeed against that kind of competition.

Transitioning from a manufacturing to a market-driven economy will not be easy nor will it be quick. But it is an obvious road that must be taken if China is to avoid what could be some very big potholes ahead.

CHAPTER
10

The Future Is Never Obvious

A search for the obvious is about today, not tomorrow. You cannot predict the future and you should never try. Today is today. Tomorrow is tomorrow.

Mispredicting the Future

Some of the most costly mistakes in business can be attributed to companies trying to predict the future. History is littered with bad predictions in all aspects of life. Here are but a few. They come from a book titled *Bad Predictions* written by Laura Lee.

Howard Rheingold, author of *Excursions to the Far Side of the Mind*, had a different view of sex in this century. "Men of the year 2000 could enjoy exotic extras like orgasmic earlobes, replaceable sex organs, ultra-sensory intercourse and a range of ecstasy options that take kinkiness to a new level." Sorry, Howard, sex still is the same old boring stuff.

Laura Lee quoted a 1979 *BusinessWeek* article that said, "With over 50 foreign cars already on sale here, the Japanese auto industry isn't likely to carve out a big slice of the U.S.

market." John Foster Dulles, in 1954, said, "The Japanese don't make anything the people in the United States would want." Sorry guys, the Japanese are killing us.

In 1974, the U.S. Forest Service published a study on "Future Leisure Environments." By 1989, it predicted private aircraft would be banned from the metropolitan airports and only nonpolluting vehicles would be allowed on the streets. Were it only so. Sorry, I still want my truck and my Gulfstream.

In 1964, Harvard Professor George Baku in an article in *New Scientist* predicted that "The more dramatic changes in products (in the next 20 years) will include such innovations as plastic houses, ultrasonic dishwashers, electronic highways and automated trains." Sorry, George, no one wants a plastic house and trains and highways have only changed for the worse.

Coca-Cola Chairman Roberto Goizueta predicted in 1985 that the New Coke would be "The most significant soft drink development in the company's history. . . . The surest move ever made." Well, Roberto, it turned out to be the most significant bomb in Coke's history.

Roger Smith, Chairman of General Motors, predicted in 1986 that "By the turn of this century, we will live in a paperless society." Roger, unfortunately, got a lot of things wrong.

Alfred L. Malabre of the *Wall Street Journal* predicted in 1966 that "The highly productive employee of 2000 will work only 37 hours or three-quarters the length of today's workweek." Alfred, I'd say that just keeping those long-hour jobs is where it's at today.

Needless to say, the point is made. You cannot predict the future and if you try, chances are you will be very wrong. So, your search for that obvious strategy should be based on what is happening today.

What makes predicting so difficult, if not impossible, are three things. First is technology. Unforeseen inventions can quickly change the status quo. Two weeks before their historical flight, Wilbur Wright said to his brother Orville, "Man will not fly for 50 years." Next is the human condition. People's habits change very slowly, which is why the future often looks like the past. Finally, competition can rear its ugly head with new ideas that disrupt old ideas.

Unfortunately, many powerful obvious ideas founder on the future.

In other words, while a company sees the value of a strategy for today's and tomorrow's business, they aren't so sure it will hold up all the way into the future. They want an idea that will be able to accommodate some future yet still unformulated plan.

Once, in a roomful of Xerox technical management people, I was pushing the future of laser printing as a big business. "Lasography" as a follow-up to "Xerography."

After the presentation, some senior engineer stood up and declared that laser printing was old hat. They had been working on it for a number of years. What they needed was an idea that encompassed the present as well as the future. When I politely asked what the future held, he proudly announced "ion deposition."

All I could say was, "Let's do Lasography today, and when you're ready you can do Ionography." (All that remark did was to make me out to be a wise-ass. End of sale.)

Finding success today is what you must first worry about. If you do that, your chances that you'll have some money to spend on tomorrow will be greatly enhanced.

One observation I've heard a lot is, "I don't want to be niched. I want to keep my future options open."

Believe me, if you don't get niched in the customer's mind, your future options will be quite limited. My advice to all those who worry about the future is simple and obvious. Today is today. Tomorrow is tomorrow and you can't plan on today looking anything like tomorrow.

And believe me, it's tough enough just to solve today's problems.

EPILOGUE

At the Heart of the Search Is the Concept of Simplicity

Through the years, being called "simple" was never a plus. And being called "simpleminded" or a "simpleton" was downright negative. It meant you were stupid, gullible, or feebleminded. It's no wonder that people fear being simple.

I call it the *curse of Simple Simon.*

When psychologists are asked about this fear, they get a little more complex. (Not surprising.) Psychologist John Collard of the Institute of Human Relations at Yale University described seven kinds of common fears and all of us have some of them:

1. Fear of failure.
2. Fear of sex.
3. Fear of self-defense.
4. Fear of trusting others.
5. Fear of thinking.
6. Fear of speaking.
7. Fear of being alone.

It would appear that not being simple—or not seeking simple solutions—stems from number 5, fear of thinking.

The problem is that instead of thinking things through for
ourselves, we rely on the thinking of others. (This is why the
worldwide management consulting business is well over $200
billion.)

Says Dr. Collard: "Not only is it hard work to think, but
many people fear the activity itself. They are docile and obe-
dient and easily follow suggestions put forward by others,
because it saves them the labor of thinking for themselves.
They become dependent on others for headwork, and fly to a
protector when in difficulty."

Susan Jacoby has written a frightening book titled *The Age
of American Unreason.* In it she writes that "our country has
become unthinking and is now ill with a powerful mutant
strain of intertwined ignorance, anti-rationalism, and anti-
intellectualism."

This fear of thinking is having a profound impact in the
business of news. Some even wonder whether it has much of a
future.

Columnist Richard Reeves suggests that "the end of news"
may be near. The avalanche of news about the rapid changes
of modern life is turning people off. Audiences "do not want
complicated and emotionally complex stories that remind
them of their own frustrations and powerlessness."

Reeves is probably right about the growing avoidance of
complexity. People don't want to think.

That's why simplicity has such power. By oversimplifying a
complex issue, you are making it easy for people to make a
decision without too much thought. Consider the complex
trial of O. J. Simpson and how Johnnie Cochran put the
essence of his argument into one memorable line: "If [the
glove] doesn't fit, you must acquit."

"Make your scandals complex and you can beat the rap every time," says speechwriter Peggy Noonan referring to Whitewater, which, unlike Watergate, lacked the easily grasped story line that people want.

But psychologist Carol Moog comes at the problem from another vantage point. She states that in our culture there's a "paranoia of omission." There's a sense that you have to cover all your options because you could be attacked at any moment. You can't miss anything or it could be fatal to your career.

In other words, if you have only one idea and that idea fails, you have no safety net. And because we are so success-driven, it magnifies the number one fear, "fear of failure."

You feel naked with a simple idea. A variety of ideas enables a person to hedge his or her bets.

Our general education and most management training teach us to deal with every variable, seek out every option, and analyze every angle. This leads to maddening complexity. And the most clever among us produce the most complex proposals and recommendations.

Unfortunately, when you start spinning out all kinds of different solutions, you're on the road to chaos. You end up with contradictory ideas and people running in different directions. Simplicity requires that you narrow the options and return to a single path.

The best way to deal with these natural fears is to focus on the problem. It's analogous to how a ballet dancer avoids getting dizzy when doing a pirouette. The trick is to focus on one object in the audience every time your head comes around.

Needless to say, you have to recognize the right problem on which to focus.

If you're Volvo, the problem on which to focus is how to maintain your leadership in the concept of "safety" as others try to jump on your idea.

That's pretty obvious.

If you're Starbucks, the problem on which to focus is how to convince your customers that your coffee is worth the money.

That's pretty obvious.

If you're a newspaper, the problem on which to focus is why people should read you and not go elsewhere for news or information.

That's pretty obvious.

If you're a conglomerate, the problem is to develop a portfolio of powerful brands or people will not know what you're about.

That's pretty obvious.

So there it is. If you are willing to use your common sense and keep things simple, you should be able to reach that obvious solution. If you can't do these things, find someone to help that can.

I would like to end with an untold story. Many years ago, I was in an IBM meeting about their corporate image. Their problem was a reputation built around mainframe computing, a concept that was being made obsolete by the rise of desktop computing. My recommendation was an obvious one. Since only IBM had underlying technology in all aspects of computing, it made sense that they were in the best position to help a customer put the pieces together into a computer system. The concept to replace mainframe computing: integrated computing.

The meeting broke up and I never found out where that recommendation went. What I do know is that, in the ensuing years, IBM executed that idea in their computer services unit, which saved IBM and made the head of the unit, Sam Palmisano, the current CEO.

It's the most visible example I know of the power of an obvious idea.

BIBLIOGRAPHY

Abrahams, Jeffery. *The Mission Statement Book*. Berkeley, CA: Ten Speed Press, 1995.

Adams, Walter, and James W. Brock. *The Bigness Complex*. Stanford, CA: Stanford University Press, 1986.

Andrew, Ferguson. "Now They Want Your Kids," *Time*, September 29, 1997.

Bullmore, Jeremy. *Marketing Magazine*.

Collins, James, and Jerry Porras. *Built to Last*. New York: HarperCollins, 1994.

Covey, Stephen. *The 7 Habits of Highly Effective Families*. New York: Free Press, 1989.

Drucker, Peter. *The Essential Drucker*. New York: Harper-Collins, 2001.

Drucker, Peter. *Seeing Things as They Really Are*. New York: Forbes, 1997.

Friedman, Thomas L. "Tone It Down a Notch. . . ." *New York Times*, October 2, 2002.

Gladwell, Malcolm. *The Tipping Point*. Boston: Little, Brown & Co., 2000.

Hammer, Michael. *The Reengineering Revolution*. Cambridge, MA: Hammer and Co., 1948.

Hammer, Michael, and Steve A. Stanton. *The Reengineering Revolution*. 2nd ed. New York: HarperCollins, 1995.

Helm, Burt. "Which Ads Don't Get Skipped?" *BusinessWeek*, September 3, 2007.

Hoffman, Bob. *The Ad Contrarian*. San Francisco: Author, 2007.

Jacoby, Susan. *The Age of American Unreason*. New York: Random House, 2008.

Kim, W. Chan., *Blue Ocean Strategy*. Boston: Harvard Business School Publishing, 2005.

Lee, Laura, *Bad Predictions*. Rochester Hills, MI: Elsewhere Press, 2000.

Mintzberg, Henry, "Musing on Management." *Harvard Business Review*, July–August, 1996.

Nocera, Joe. "The Case of the Subpar Smartphone." *New York Times*, September 8, 2007.

Osborn, Alex F. *Applied Imagination*. New York: Charles Scribner & Sons, 1955.

Penn, Mark. *Microtrends*. New York: Twelve, 2007.

Peter, Lawrence J., and Raymond Hull. *The Peter Principle*. New York: William Morrow, 1979.

Peters, Tom. *In Search of Excellence*. New York: Harper-Collins, 1982.

Petty, Richard, and John Cacioppo, *Attitude and Persuasion*. Boulder, CO: Westview Press, 1996.

Porter, Michael E. *On Competition*. Boston: Harvard Business School Publishing, 1979.

Rheingold, Howard. *Excursions to the Far Side of the Mind*. New York: Beech Tree Books, 1989.

Ries, Al, and Jack Trout. *Marketing Warfare*. New York: McGraw-Hill, 1986.

Ries, Al, and Jack Trout. *Marketing Warfare*. 20th anniversary ed. New York: McGraw-Hill, 2000.

Ries, Al, and Jack Trout. *Positioning: The Battle for Your Mind*. New York: McGraw-Hill, 1981.

Ries, Al, and Jack Trout. *The 22 Immutable Laws of Marketing.* New York: HarperCollins, 1993.

Roberts, Kevin. *Lovemarks: The Future Beyond Brands.* Brooklyn, NY: powerHouse Books, 2004.

Shenk, David, *Data Smog.* New York: HarperOne, 1997.

Trout, Jack. *Big Brands. Big Trouble.* New York: John Wiley & Sons, 2001.

Trout, Jack, with Steve Rivkin. *Differentiate or Die.* New York: John Wiley & Sons, 2000.

Trout, Jack, with Steve Rivkin. *Differentiate or Die.* 2nd ed. Hoboken, NJ: John Wiley & Sons, 2008.

Trout, Jack, with Steve Rivkin. *The New Positioning.* New York: McGraw-Hill, 1996.

Updegraff, Robert R. *Obvious Adams: The Story of a Successful Businessman.* Louisville, KY: Updegraff Press, 1953.

INDEX

A

Absolut Vodka, 79
Acura, 156
Adapting ideas, 116
Advertising, 39–56
  awards, 55, 56
  candor in, 76
  creativity trap, 50–55, 75
  defined, 53
  differentiating idea and,
    90–91
  emotions and, 42–46
  evaluating, 75–77
  fixing the industry, 55–56
  money spent on, 149
  sloganeering, 46–55
  Super Bowl, 39–40, 90, 148
  as theater, 39–42
Advertising Age, 89–90
AFLAC, 53
Air Force, 107
Alka-Seltzer, 53
American Airlines, 79
American Express, 50
American Motors, 136
A&M Pet Products, 149
Anheuser-Busch, 37, 40, 58, 165
Antarctica beer, 109–110
Apple Computer, 61–62, 62,
    148
Aquafina, 76
Arm & Hammer, 117
Arrogance, 126
Association of Advertising, 75

AT&T, 61, 97, 127
Attitudes and Persuasion (Petty
    and Cacioppo), 83
Attribute sacrifice, 89
Automobile industry. *See also*
    specific companies
  differentiation in,
    37–38
  going up-market, 171–172,
    173–174
  Law of Division, 133,
    134–136
  Law of Duality, 146
  Law of Perception,
    139–141
  Law of Singularity, 142–143
  predictions, bad, 187–188
Averages, Law of, 141–142
Avis, 50, 80, 98

B

Bad Predictions (Lee), 187–188
Baku, George, 188
Ban deodorant, 96
Banks, 37, 52
Beer industry, 40, 134, 158,
    164–166. *See also specific*
    companies
Behavioral targeting, 36–38
Bernbach, Bill, 76
BIC, 59, 100
Big, as enemy of obvious,
    121–124
BlackBerry, 62

Block, Ryan, 62
Blue Moon Brewing Co., 165
BMW, 56, 64, 65, 95, 103
Boar's Head, 76
Boeing, 68, 106–107
Bowflex, 46
Brabeck, Peter, 57
Brahma beer, 109–110
Branding:
    brand names, 84–85
    defined, 86
    differentiating idea and,
        37–38, 85–86
    internal forces that unravel,
        87–88
    sacrifice and, 88–89
Brand schizophrenia, 63–65
Branson, Richard, 170–171
Bryant, Kobe, 163
Budweiser, 37, 111, 158, 165
Buffett, Warren, 159
Buick, 134–135, 151, 152, 153,
    162
Built to Last (Collins and
    Porras), 68
Bullmer, Jeremy, 106
Burger King, 35, 97, 145
Bush, George W., 96, 104
Business school education,
    9–10
Buyers, risks to, 113
Buzz factor, 40–41

C
Cacioppo, John, 83
Cadillac:
    brand schizophrenia, 152
    going up-market, 171
    Law of Division, 134–136
    leadership, 114
    models, 7–8, 87

Candor in advertising, 76
Cannes advertising awards, 55,
    56
Canon, 120, 121
Cantalupo, Jim, 16
Cardin, Pierre, 169–170
Caress bath soap, 85
Carnegie, Dale, 117–118
Carrier Air Conditioning,
    175–176
Catalogs, 91
CBS, 78, 134
Celebrities, 161–163
CEOs (chief executive officers),
    11–15
Chandler, Susan, 169
Change:
    coping with, 118–121
    customer resistance to,
        80–84
Cheerios, 101
Chevrolet:
    brand schizophrenia, 153
    customer perception, 7–8
    Law of Division, 133,
        134–135
    Law of Singularity, 143
    sales leadership, 110
Chief executive officers (CEOs),
    11–15
China, 184–186
Chrysler, 110, 111–112, 146
CIA, 107
Cigarette smoking, 181–182
Cirque du Soleil, 117
Citigroup, 121–122
Clio awards, 56
Coca-Cola:
    advertising, 43
    brand identity, 153
    brand schizophrenia, 64, 65

Law of Duality, 145–146
Law of Perception, 140
Law of Singularity,
    143–144
leadership claim, 109
logo, 80
predictions, bad, 188
tinkering, 156–158
"Cocktail party problem," 175
Coke. *See* Coca-Cola
Colgate, 111, 145
Collard, John, 191–192
Collins, James, 68
Color in logos, 79–80
Combining ideas, 116
Commoditization, 37–38,
    85–86, 167
Common sense, 6–10, 20
Communications devices,
    28–31
Competition:
    coping with, 96–102
    repositioning, 93–96
Competitive mental angle,
    72–73
Confucius, 129–130
Conglomerates, 121–124,
    174–176, 194
Consignia, 85
Context, making sense in, 69
Continental Airlines, 45
Convergence, 61–63
Coors, 165
Corning, 110
Corona beer, 40
Corporate identity, 59, 77–80
CORT furniture company, 46
Corvette, 89
Cosmetics, 43
Coupons, 81
Covey, Stephen, 7

Craftsman, 160, 176, 177
Creativity trap in advertising,
    50–55, 75
Credit cards, 37, 42–43
Crest toothpaste, 53, 97, 111,
    145
Crocker, Betty, 163
Cross-tabulations, 22
"Cupboard of the Future,"
    5–6
Curves workout facilities, 117
Customers:
    awareness versus behavior, 21
    resistance to change,
        80–84
    satisfaction studies, 22
Cynicism, 10

D
Daimler Benz, 59
DEC, 97, 102, 127
Dell, 81, 89, 153
DeWalt, 89
DieHard batteries, 85, 160, 177
Differentiating idea:
    advertising and, 90–91
    branding and, 37–38,
        85–86
    communicating, 70–71
    credentials to support, 70
    described, 72–73
    finding, 69–70
    turning into strategy, 73–75
Direction versus solutions,
    102–105
Disruptive technologies,
    127–128
Distraction factor, 133
Division, Law of, 133–136
Dominican Republic tourism
    ads, 46

Drucker, Peter, 26, 67, 68, 185
Drug usage, reducing,
    180–184
Duality, Law of, 112–113,
    144–147
Dulles, John Foster, 188
Dunbar, Robin, 123
Dunkin' Donuts, 166, 167
Duracell, 63, 88, 111, 145

E
Ear, Law of the, 129–133
Eastman, George, 118–119
Economists, 8–9
Edison, Thomas, 115
Ego, 10
E-mail, 28–31
Emerson, Ralph Waldo, 6, 77
Emotions, 42–46
"Everybody knows" principle,
    140–141
Everything-for-everybody trap,
    126–127
"Evident speech," 2
Explosions, mental, 4–5

F
Fears, common, 191–192
Federal Express, 79, 80
Fidelity Investments, 109
Fisher, George, 12
Ford Explorer, 110
Ford Motor Company:
    improving borrowed ideas,
        117
    Law of Division, 133
    Law of Duality, 146
    Law of Singularity, 143
    leadership position, 111–112
Friedman, Milton, 15
Friedman, Thomas, 160, 179

Fuji Photo, 80, 119–120, 145
Future, 187–190

G
Gadgets, 18–19
Galbraith, John Kenneth, 82
Galvanic skin response test,
    22–23
Garner, James, 163
Gatorade, 40
GE. *See* General Electric (GE)
GEICO, 53
General Electric (GE):
    big as enemy of obvious, 121,
        123, 124
    business names, 176
    competitors, 100–101
    goals, 68
    leadership position, 112
    logo, 78, 80
    marketing strategy versus
        employee focus, 20
    Six Sigma, 136
General Motors (GM):
    arrogance, 126
    brand schizophrenia, 13, 63,
        151–153, 154
    common sense, 7–8
    competitors, 100
    customer awareness versus
        behavior, 21
    goals, 74
    improving borrowed ideas,
        117
    Law of Division, 135–136
    Law of Duality, 146
    Law of Resources, 149
    Law of Singularity, 142–143
    leadership position,
        111–112
    reliability message, 126

repositioning, 103–104
simplicity, 2–3
Gillette, 100
Gladwell, Malcolm, 123
GM. *See* General Motors (GM)
Goals, 73–74
Goizueta, Roberto, 188
Golden Cat Corporation, 149
Google, 144, 147
Gore-Tex, 17
Graham, Donald, 159
Greensburg, Jack, 16
Green Valley Brewing Co.,
    165
Groupware, 14
Grove, Andy, 19
Growth, 17–18

H
Haas, Jeffrey, 28–29
Hammer, Michael, 83
Harley-Davidson, 140
Harvard Business Review, 165
Hasbro Inc., 171
Heclo, Hugh, 30–31
Heinz, 59, 88, 109
Helm, Bruce, 46
Herd effect, 48, 113–114
Hershey's, 109
Hertz, 79, 80, 98, 111
Hewlett-Packard, 120, 121
Hingis, Martina, 163
Holiday Inn Crowne
    Plaza, 87
Home Depot, 86, 136, 137
Honda, 139–140, 155–156
Hooters Restaurant, 46
Hull, Raymond, 12
Human nature, conformity
    with, 3–4
Hyundai, 173–174

I
IBM:
    arrogance, 126
    competitors, 102
    corporate image, 194
    differentiating idea, 51
    goals, 68
    Law of Division, 134
    leadership claim, 109
    logo, 79, 80
    purchase of Lotus
        Development
        Corporation, 14
Ideas, borrowing, 115–118
Information overload, 20, 25–30
Initials as company name/
    nickname, 80, 84
Innovation, 185–186
In Search of Excellence (Peters),
    68
Intel, 18–19
Intellectual subtlety, 9
Intensive Care skin lotion, 85
Internet, 25–38
    behavioral targeting, 36–38
    e-mail, 28–31
    information overload, 25–28
    print catalogs and, 91
    Web-based campaigns, 40–41
    when no one is in charge,
        89–90
    word-of-mouth marketing,
        31–36
iPhone, 62
iPod, 114, 116
Iraq, 104

J
Jacob Leinenkugel Brewing
    Company, 164–165
Jacoby, Susan, 192

Jaguar automobile, 79
James, William, 25
Jordan, Michael, 161–162

K
Kelleher, Herb, 14–15, 101
Kellogg's cornflakes, 101
Kenmore, 160, 176, 177
Kerry, John, 96
Kettering, Charles F., 2–3
Kevin, Robert, 42
KFC, 88
Kia, 173–174
King Kong, 32
Kmart, 177
Kodak, 12, 80, 118–121, 127,
    145
Krispy Kreme, 15

L
Lagasse, Emeril, 161, 162
Lampert, Edward, 176, 178
Landor, Walter, 84
Law of Averages, 141–142
Law of Division, 133–136
Law of Duality, 112–113,
    144–147
Law of Line Extension, 140
Law of Perception, 136–141
Law of Resources, 34,
    147–150
Law of Singularity, 141–144
Law of the Ear, 129–133
Lawrence, Mary Wells, 146, 154
Leadership, 108–115
Lee, Laura, 187–188
Lenovo, 186
Lenzing, 110
Leonardo da Vinci, 8
Levi's, 97, 101
Levitz Furniture, 107

Lexus, 153, 155–156, 172
Licensing, 168–171
Light, Larry, 64–65
Lincoln, Abraham, 6–7
Line extension, 126–127, 140
Listening, 10
Listerine, 95, 145
Loftus, Elizabeth, 131
Logos, 59, 77–80
Lotus Development
    Corporation, 14
Lowe's, 45, 117, 136

M
Macy's, 161, 162–163, 170
Malabre, Alfred L., 188
Manzi, Jim, 14
Marketing:
    complexity in, 71–72
    essence of, 72
    importance of, 67–68
    mistakes, 124–128
    steps in process, 69–71
    when no one is in charge,
        89–91
    word-of-mouth, 31–36
Markkula, Mike, 148
Marlboro, 64, 87, 111, 120, 153
Marquis by Waterford, 87
MasterCard, 42–43
McCartney, Stella, 169
McDonald's:
    advertising, 48, 108
    brand schizophrenia,
        64–65
    celebrities and, 163
    coffee, 166, 167
    Law of Duality, 145
    strength, 16, 97
    tinkering factor, 58
Media factor, 40

Mercedes:
  branding, 87
  brand schizophrenia, 63–64
  differentiating idea, 103
  Law of Division, 135, 136
  logo, 78
  rationalization for cost,
    166–167
  reliability message, 126
  repositioned by BMW, 95
Me-too mistake, 125, 126
Metropolitan Life Insurance,
  80
Microsoft, 14, 100, 144, 147
Miller Beer, 158, 164–165
Milliken, 17
Mindray Medical International,
  186
Mintzberg, Henry, 8
Mission statements,
  105–108
Mistakes, marketing,
  124–128
Mobil, 79
Molson Coors Brewing Co.,
  165
Moog, Carol, 193
Motorola Q, 62
MP3 craze, 114
MTV, 80–81
Murdoch, Rupert, 158, 170
Murrow, Edward R., 35
Museum of Paleontology
    (University of California
    at Berkeley), 115–116
MySpace, 81

N
Names, company/brand,
  84–85
Nardelli, Bob, 136, 137

Nash Rambler, 136
Nestle, 57–58
Neuroscience, 22
New Coke, 64, 140, 188
Newspaper industry, 158–161,
  194
Newton, 61–62
New York Life, 80
New York Times, 159, 160
New Zealand tourism
  marketing, 60
Nike, 78, 88, 114, 145,
  161–162, 163
Nikon, 120
Nissan, 139
Nocera, Joe, 62
Nokia, 48, 108
Noonan, Peggy, 193
Nordstrom, 89, 163
NutraSweet, 85

O
Obvious, defined, 2
Obvious Adams (Updegraff),
  1–6
Obviousness tests, 2–6
Off-road vehicles, 9, 114
Okidata's Doc-it, 61
Oldsmobile, 134–135, 153
Otis Elevator, 123,
  175–176

P
Packard, David, 68
Packard cars, 173
Palmisano, Sam, 194
Palm's Treo, 62
Papa John's Pizza, 73, 89
Passikoff, Robert, 21–23
Pelosi, Nancy, 19, 96
Penn, Mark, 45–46

Pepsi-Cola:
    advertising for Aquafina, 76
    customer resistance to
        change, 82
    Law of Duality, 145–146
    Law of Singularity, 143
    logo, 80
    radio commercial, 131
    sacrifice, 89
Perception, 125–126,
    136–141
Performance leadership, 111
Perot, Ross, 10
Peter, Lawrence, 12
Peter Principle, The (Peter and
    Hull), 12
Peters, Tom, 68
Petty, Richard, 83
Playskool diapers, 171
Pontiac, 32–33, 36, 55,
    134–135, 151, 153
Porras, Jerry, 68
Porsche, 111, 153
Porter, Michael, 86
Pratt & Whitney Corporation,
    168, 175–176
Predictions, bad, 187–188
Prell Shampoo, 58, 82
Procter & Gamble:
    emotional connection with
        customers, 42, 43
    Law of Duality, 146
    Law of Resources, 149
    repositioning the
        competition, 95
    research, 21
    slice-of-life approach, 133
Products, multifunctional,
    61–63
Product sacrifice, 88
Publicity, cost of, 148

Q
Quiksilver, 44, 114

R
Reading, 26, 27–28
Reebok, 145, 163
Reengineering Revolution, The
    (Hammer), 83
Reeves, Richard, 192
Research, 21–23
Resources, Law of, 34, 147–150
Rheingold, Howard, 187
Riggio, Len, 27
Roehm, Julie, 154–155
Rolex, 43, 167
Rove, Karl, 96
Royal Crown cola, 145–146
Royal Mail Group, 85

S
Sacrifice, 60–61, 88–89
Sales leadership, 110
Sam Adams beer, 40
Santayana, George, 152
Saturn automobiles, 117
Saussure, Ferdinand de, 132
Schnatter, John, 73
Schultz, Howard, 166, 167, 168
Scoop Away, 149
Scope mouthwash, 95, 145
Seagram, 34, 108
Sears, 126, 160, 176–178
Segmentation studies, 21–22
Segway, 32
Shenk, David, 26
Simon, Paul, 115
Simplicity, 2–3
Simpson, Jessica, 161, 162
Singularity, Law of, 141–144
Six Sigma, 136, 137
SKF, 51

Sloan, Alfred, 103, 152
Sloganeering, runaway,
    46–55
Smartphones, 62
Smirnoff, 33–35, 95
Smith, Roger, 74, 188
Snakes on a Plane, 35–36
Social capacity, 123
Soft drink industry, 40, 133,
    140, 145–146. *See also*
    specific companies
Solutions versus direction,
    102–105
Sono-Site, 100–101
Sony, 116, 120, 121
Sorrell, Martin, 44
Sound, importance of,
    129–133
Southwest Airlines, 14–15, 88,
    101, 156
Starbucks, 166–168, 194
Stewart, Martha, 161, 162, 177
Stolichnaya, 95
Strategy, 73–75
Substituting, 116
Super Bowl ads, 39–40, 90, 148
SUV craze, 114, 117

T
Target market sacrifice, 89
Target stores, 153, 155, 163,
    171, 172
Technology, 110, 127–128
Television industry, 134
Thinking:
    time for, 18–20
    wishful, 10
3M Company, 80
Thurman, Uma, 170
Tico fisherman story, 17–18
Tide detergent, 42, 43

Tidy Cat, 149
Tidy Scoop, 149
Time, 89–90
Timeliness, 5–6
Tinkering factor, 57–60
Tipping Point, The (Gladwell),
    123
Titleist, 109, 162
TiVo, 46, 50
Toyota:
    branding, 155–156, 172
    differentiating idea, 85, 97,
        103, 126, 153
    Law of Duality, 146
    Law of Perception, 139
    leadership position, 112
    sales leadership, 110, 151
Treo, 62
Trump, Donald, 161, 162, 170
Truth, 125–126
Tsingtao beer, 185
Twain, Mark, 23
Tylenol, 94–95

U
Unique selling proposition, 55
United Technologies,
    175–176
University of California at
    Berkeley Museum of
    Paleontology, 115–116
Updegraff, Robert, 1–6, 137
U.S. Forest Service, 188
U.S. State Department,
    178–180

V
Viacom, 80–81
Viagra, 145
Vick, Michael, 163
Virgin brand, 170–171

Visa, 42–43, 50
Visual chauvinism, 129
Visual ethnology, 22
Volkswagen (VW):
    Beetle, 73, 76
    customer resistance to
        change, 82
    Law of Division, 135
    Phaeton, 59, 171–172
    strategy, 74
Volvo, 53, 60–61, 88, 105, 193
VW. *See* Volkswagen (VW)

W
Wall Street, 15–18, 127
Wall Street Journal, 158, 159,
    160
Wal-Mart:
    advertising, 45
    brand identity, 153, 154–155,
        156
    commoditization, 86
    competitors, 100
    cost leadership, 42, 171, 172
    differentiating idea, 163
    goals, 68
Washington Post, 159, 160
Waterford Crystal, 87

Weatherbeater, 160, 177
Welch, Jack, 112, 136, 146
Western Union, 81–82
Whole Foods, 43–44
Windex, 85
Wishful thinking, 10
Woods, Tiger, 162
Word-of-mouth marketing,
    31–36
Words, importance of, 129–133
Wright, Orville, 189
Wright, Wilbur, 189
Writing, 4

X
Xerox:
    customer resistance to
        change, 82
    disruptive technologies,
        127
    future directions, 189
    leadership claim, 109
    logo redesign, 59
    office of the future, 9

Y
Yahoo, 144, 147
YouTube, 81